Model Scenic Railways
Design and construction

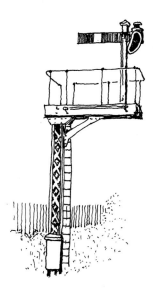

Robert F. Brien

Model Scenic Railways

Design and construction

B.T. Batsford Ltd, London

ISBN 0 7134 5589 6

Typeset by Tameside Filmsetting, Ltd.
and printed in Great Britain by
The Bath Press Ltd
Bath, Somerset
for the publishers
B.T. Batsford Ltd
4 Fitzhardinge Street
London
WIH OAH

for
Ray Cockcroft,
my father-in-law,
who was there at the beginning

Contents

Acknowledgements

The author and publishers would like to thank Peco Products and Publications for their kind cooperation in providing many of the photographs, especially Mr S. C. Pritchard, the managing editor, for his helpful advice and comments and Messrs Lloyd and Irving. Thanks are also extended to manufacturers and others who provided photographs and information towards the compilation of the book: Gaugemaster, Graham Farish, Linka System, Ratio Plastic Models Limited, Riko International Limited, and the National Railway Museum in York. The remaining photographs were taken by the author, and he is indebted to Alan Southgate of Harpenden for his advice and for processing the results.

Cover illustration courtesy of Hornby Hobbies Ltd.

Introduction

Model railways in a great diversity of forms can rightly be described as one of the most widespread and popular hobbies. It appeals to all ages and levels of society, and the direction of its appeal has the most surprising number of variations. There are still those who think of model railways as no more than toy trains, and tend to refer rather disparagingly to 'Uncle's train set' in the loft. Yet the hobby has progressed a long way since the original concept of a train set. This was no more than an oval of interconnected rails on the bedroom carpet, with a tinplate clockwork (or later, electric) engine pulling a few coaches, which was hastily dismantled and tossed into the toy-cupboard at bedtime. The major change has been the transformation into a layout by the inclusion of realistic landscaping and model buildings to give a comprehensive display of an operating railway in a complete setting.

The great variations in the hobby come from each individual's emphasis on the particular aspects that have the most appeal for him. There are those for whom the ideal is a perfect scale model of a section of an actual railway, often from the past, which not only looks exactly as the original, but is operated on a precise, if condensed, version of the real timetable. These perfectionists derive considerable pleasure from careful research and meticulous construction of the buildings, scenery, locomotives and rolling stock. Nostalgia often plays an important part, a not unreasonable yearning for the days of the steam train, which, viewed from the aspect of today's troubled times, seem to have possessed a quality of tranquillity, care and dependability long since obsolete.

Then there are those who are simply fascinated by the world of models, and model trains in particular. The incredible degree of detail that present-day technology allows on scale models and the realism in the operation of moving parts is a source of wonder and continual pleasure. To these enthusiasts the importance of realism in railway liveries or the accuracy of timetables is secondary. On their layouts a German express locomotive pulling a set of GWR coaches may run happily beside a Canadian Pacific engine drawing a LNER train. There is the story of a man who observed that only one side of his train was visible as it ran round the continuous circuit in his loft. He therefore decided to paint the other side with a different livery, so that when run in the opposite direction an entirely different train could be seen!

It seems then that model railways can be 'all things to all men' – or women, for that matter – and this in itself makes the hobby unique. You may possess endless patience, you may be ham-fisted, you may only have a few precious hours a week to devote to your hobby; whatever your circumstances, you will find an area of this intriguing pastime that will accommodate *you*. And only you can

1 Culmhidon Station, with the town in the
background beyond the bridge and the goods
yard on the right. This is part of the author's
extensive loft layout.

decide the direction in which you want to develop your talents and interest. Convention need not influence this decision. Your satisfaction may derive more from the construction than from the operation of the completed system, in which case you will need to plan a long-term development. You may find that you have a flair for landscaping, or some hidden architectural talent may reveal itself in the buildings you design. Whatever you choose you can be sure that you have before you many years of relaxation and pleasure and the satisfaction of a well-chosen hobby.

This book deals with the types of layout and the selection of a suitable location to accommodate the one chosen. Details are given of the methods of setting out and laying trackwork, and the installation of circuits for the control of trains, signals and lighting, including fully automatic control. Methods of constructing scenery, landscapes and buildings from raw materials as well as from kits are covered to suit varying degrees of dexterity. Rolling stock in various forms, including kits and ready-to-run models, is described in the final section; and the suppliers' list deals with sources from which some of the less readily available materials described in the text may be obtained.

1 Preliminary considerations

As with most projects, taking a little time at the very outset to consider what it is you are attempting to achieve will save much time, frustration and expense at a later stage. Your enthusiasm may have been fired by a visit to an exhibition, or you may have seen a friend's layout, or simply read a book on the subject. You may be drawn to the fellowship of a local model railway club, which is ideal for someone who has little space to spare for the demands of a layout, or finds the cost beyond his means. Whatever your reasons, now is the time to make the first decision: is it to be a portable, fold-away or permanent layout? Linked with this must be the careful consideration of where the layout is to be accommodated, and how much disruption is likely to be entailed in creating this new space.

The whole concept of the layout will be greatly influenced by one vital factor: your primary interest in the subject. Is it model-making, or the running of a miniature railway system? If the former, you will need to prepare a long-term plan that you can work on for a number of years, watching it gradually grow, and perhaps never being really finished. If the latter, you may want to get down a substantial amount of trackwork fairly promptly, with only the minimum of basic landscaping and buildings as a background. It may be that your interest lies somewhere between these two limits. Thinking it over will surely be worth while in the interests of the final result.

Portable layout

This type of layout is used where it is the intention to transport the entire model occasionally to exhibitions for display purposes. It is generally employed by clubs, although there is no reason why an individual should not adopt the same idea. The layout is built on a series of robust baseboards on some form of supporting trestles, with suitable linking devices to lock the sections together accurately. The size of each section must be considered in relation to the type of vehicle that is to be used for transportation and exhibition access routes as well as storage of the dismantled layout. It will need to be rather more strongly built than other layouts, and it is essential to protect the delicate buildings, trees and landscape, both during transport and in store. Finally some form of dust-proofing is needed, as much of the completed model will be difficult to clean without causing damage.

The materials from which you construct your baseboard, either fibreboard or chipboard, are generally manufactured in 8ft × 4ft (2400mm × 1200mm) sheets, which are of course much too large and heavy for a portable layout. However, these sheets can economically be reduced in size to 4ft × 2ft (1200mm × 600mm), which seems to be the optimum size for each section. The method of construction of these units is described on page 27.

Fold-away layout

An ideal location for your layout may be available, but the space could be too valuable to permit its permanent allocation for this use. In this instance you might consider the fold-away layout, which may be constructed in a sun porch, a bedroom, garage or other area that will serve a dual function. At the end of a modelling or operating session the entire layout is simply hinged away to one side, and any supporting legs neatly folded on to the underside of the baseboard. The system has the advantage of keeping the layout in one piece, thus avoiding the necessity of linking devices. However, there is a limitation on the heights to which scenery or track gradients can be taken to avoid excessive thickness of the construction when not in use. Of course, it is essential to remove and store all rolling stock and unfixed items before folding the layout away, and this storage is another matter to be considered.

Permanent layout

Ultimately the best solution, if space permits, is the permanent layout. It can be sturdily constructed to the right degree of rigidity, and once fixed need not be disturbed again. Bear in mind, though, that moving house may be a reason for dismantling the layout at some future time, and if there is a possibility of moving it with you, then appropriate measures must be taken at the construction stage. Some time ago an advertisement appeared in a modelling magazine on the following lines:

> FOR SALE: Extensive model railway loft layout including landscaping, buildings, trackwork etc: £60000. Price includes semi-det 3 bedrm house with all mod cons.

The size of the layout can vary from a modest shelf around two or three walls of a bedroom to an extensive loft given over exclusively to the hobby. A little-used spare bedroom or a disused garage or shed can often provide the necessary accommodation.

If you decide to go to the trouble of allocating space permanently for your hobby, then an important factor is temperature control. Standing in a freezing garage in mid-winter trying to operate protesting locomotives will not promote enthusiasm, nor will modelling in the stifling heat of an unventilated and insulated lost. Yet overcoming these disadvantages can take a considerable amount of capital expense, and additional heating will carry its corresponding revenue costs.

Adapting your loft

Many houses and bungalows in Britain designed with the commonly encountered steep roof have a large proportion of their total volume given over to loft space. This is often wasted or used as a home for paraphenalia that could probably be removed without noticeable loss. It is certainly worth giving your loft a close inspection to see whether all or part of it might be adapted to suit the needs of a model railway layout.

The problem you are most likely to encounter is the disposition of the roof-supporting timbers. Sometimes the proliferation of these is such that the roof space

2 An example of a fold-away layout in a sun-porch extension. The clever use of a mirror helps to create an illusion of space. Storage for rolling stock is provided in the cupboards below the layout. (*Courtesy of Peco Studios*)

3 An N gauge layout around three walls of a boy's bedroom allows a considerable amount of trackwork to be used without encroaching too much into the other functions of the room. (*Courtesy of Peco Studios*)

4 This 4ft × 2ft (1200mm × 600mm) N gauge layout has found a home in one of those 'spare corners' which can sometimes be set aside in an under-used part of a house. (*Courtesy of Peco Studios*)

5 This garden shed provides an ideal location for an OO gauge model railway. The layout has good natural lighting as well as fluorescent fittings, and there is space to work as well as storage below the baseboards. (*Courtesy of Peco Studios*)

6 An excellent permanent layout located in a loft. There is a dormer window, which affords both natural light and ventilation, and full use has been made of the space available. The model room has been fully lined with insulation board for use all the year round. (*Courtesy of Peco Studios*)

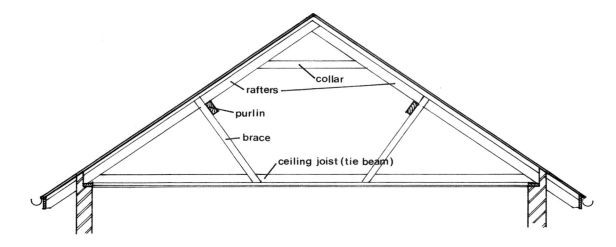

7 A common form of roof construction that would allow space for a permanent layout. The centre section could be floored, and the baseboards fitted on either side below the purlins. If the collar is too low for comfortable headroom, some form of padding should be applied to prevent accidents.

really is unusable; but often you will find that the braces and ties are such that they offer only limited obstruction. A common form of construction is shown in figure 7, where a long *purlin* supports the roof *rafters*, and this in turn is supported on *braces* at intervals, set at right angles to the roof slope. There will probably also be a *collar* at high level between the rafters. The horizontal *ceiling joists* (or *tie beams*) span across the whole roof at the same centres as the rafters. You must decide if the way these members are disposed seems to allow reasonable free space for the construction of your layout. If not, you must not under any circumstances consider removing or adjusting any of the roof timbers, or you may be faced with the expense of replacing a collapsed roof. You may invite the opinion of your local architect or builder; but generally roofs are designed economically, with every part of the construction serving a useful function.

You must also look at the ceiling joists. These already carry the weight of the ceiling below, and if they are now to support in addition the floor of your model room as well as the layout itself they must be adequately sized. Much will depend on the amount of intermediate support given by walls below, and if these occur reasonably frequently so that long spans are avoided then the usual 4in × 2in (100mm × 50mm) may be enough. But before you do any work in this connection, it is advisable to seek professional advice.

If you find that all is in order, then a $\frac{3}{4}$in (19mm) chipboard floor may be laid over the part you intend to use. The 8ft × 4ft (2400mm × 1200mm) boards will probably have to be cut in half lengthwise to get them through the access trap. They must be laid so that end joints occur over the centre of the ceiling joists, and fixed with 2in (50mm) oval nails. Flooring quality chipboard is available, which has a tongue on two edges and a groove on the other two, enabling them to be slotted together firmly without any 'give'. Take great care that you do not interfere with the electrical wiring you encounter lying on the ceiling, and if necessary allow access holes to points which may need occasional attention.

Loft insulation

Most lofts in Britain are now insulated in recognition of the energy crisis, and the most common form of insulation is fibreglass quilting. This is generally obtained in 16in (400mm) wide rolls, which fit conveniently between the ceiling joists. In using the loft as your model room you will want the barrier between the house and outside temperatures to occur above rather than below you, and this can be achieved by relocating the fibreglass. You will of course need an additional quantity of fibreglass to run up one slope and down the other instead of simply across the loft. The fibreglass is simply pushed up into the spaces between the rafters where it will remain because of the roughness of the timber. See that you enclose totally the space you wish to use, as otherwise expensive heat loss will occur. Ceiling boards can then be fixed across the rafters to complete the insulation, but one important factor must not be overlooked: the underside of the black roofing felt seen immediately above the rafters will be cold in winter. The fibreglass, being permeable, will allow warm, moist air from the house to meet this cold surface and cause condensation. It is essential to prevent this by fixing a *vapour barrier* of thin polythene sheeting across the underside of the rafters before the ceiling board is put in place (see figure 8).

Heating, ventilation and lighting

The relocation of the fibreglass insulating material allows the loft to attain a temperature similar to that of the house below, particularly when the access trap is open. Conversely, in the summer the heat of the external roof will be transferred much more slowly, giving an acceptable working temperature in the loft. Some form of ventilation is desirable, and if the house has a gable wall at the end of the loft, an airbrick in this may be enough. An adjustable grille or *register* fitted internally will enable you to close off the airbrick when necessary. Finally, good lighting in the form of spotlights or fluorescent fittings should be installed to give the best lighting conditions for the layout.

The measures described so far may be carried out without reference to local authorities, but it is essential that work such as forming openings for airbricks, and the installation of lighting and power outlets, is carried out by a competent, qualified person. When major changes are carried out, such as fitting a window or dormer to the loft, your local council become involved, and approvals must be sought. The loft will then become a *habitable space*, and will be subject to a rating charge, which will of course have a long-term effect on the overall cost of your hobby.

8 A method of insulating the roof space on the slope. The vapour barrier between the insulation board and the underside of the rafters is essential to prevent condensation and subsequent damage to the roof timbers.

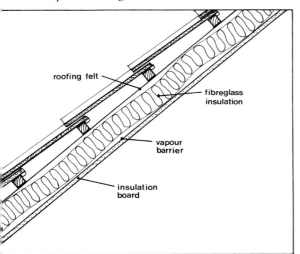

roofing felt

fibreglass insulation

vapour barrier

insulation board

Planning

Everything so far indicates that considerable care must be taken in choosing the type and location of your layout. Having come to a decision, there are still matters to which some thought must be given before you make a start. The first of these is to prepare a plan of your layout making the very best use of the space available. Almost certainly you will want to construct your model in stages although eagerness to see things happening might induce you to lay the baseboards and track and get the trains running before you make a start on landscaping. Whatever you decide, be determined to have a final plan before the first baseboard frame is fixed in position. Plaster scenery is difficult to remodel, and trackwork and turnouts do not take kindly to being torn up and relaid, particularly if ballasted.

Selection of gauge

The most popular gauge for railway modellers is at present OO, which is equivalent to a scale of 4mm to 1ft. Closely associated with it is HO gauge, the Continental version of OO, at 3.5mm to 1ft. Because of the small difference between the two, track gauge has been rationalised to one size (16.5mm) and this is referred to as OO/HO. This small difference, however, is significant. For example, if you populate the streets of your OO gauge model with HO figures, there is an unmistakable smallness about them which never looks quite right. A 6ft man to OO gauge stands 24mm high, while to HO gauge he would only be 21mm, a difference of almost 1ft in reality.

Manufacturers provide a wealth of items to suit these two scales, from locomotives and rolling stock to building kits and trackside accessories. The choice is considerable. This very convenient scale is sufficiently small to allow extensive layouts in confined spaces, with fairly realistic track radii, while still allowing the reproduction of minute and accurate detail on models.

The next scale down is N gauge, which is almost half the size of OO gauge, at 2.062mm to 1ft. In recent years this has become very popular with modellers, mainly because four times as much landscape and trackwork can be accommodated in the same space as an OO gauge layout. However, on these tiny models scale is inevitably a problem. Valve gear on a locomotive, if correctly scaled down, becomes extremely flimsy. Manufacturers, therefore, tend to make them more robust by building them a little larger than scale size. This is not to say that all N gauge products are out of scale, for there are many ingenious compromises in the design of these tiny items. The professional modeller's rule is that if it can be seen then it should be modelled to scale; so if you are going to be particular about scale perhaps you should consider a larger gauge.

Even smaller is the comparatively recently-introduced Z gauge, at 1.5mm to 1ft. This would appear to have insurmountable scale restrictions, and must surely be too small for the railway modeller to consider seriously. One hears of trendy businessmen pulling out a drawer in their desks to reveal a complete working model railway layout – but perhaps this underlines the suspicion that Z gauge is no more than an executive toy.

At the other end of the scale, at almost twice the size of OO gauge, is O gauge, at 7mm to 1ft; and this is followed by 1 gauge which is 10mm to 1ft. At these scales the difficulties of reproducing tiny details are much reduced, and beside their smaller counterparts these models appear substantial and realistic. The smallest practical size at which live steam models may be constructed

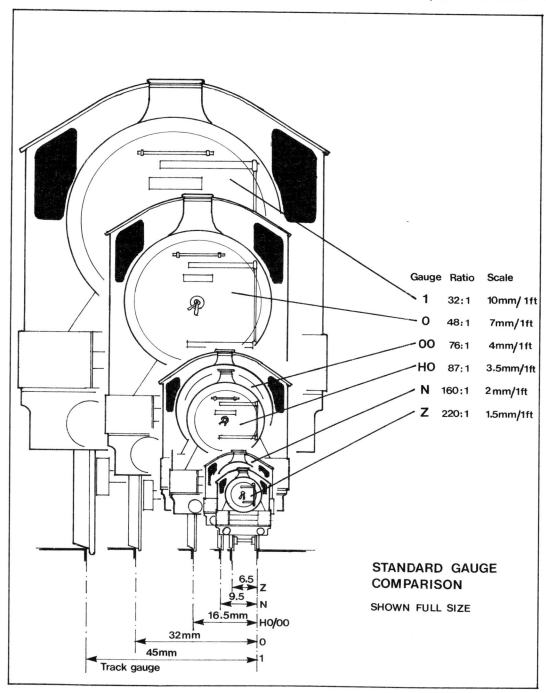

Gauge	Ratio	Scale
1	32:1	10mm/1ft
O	48:1	7mm/1ft
OO	76:1	4mm/1ft
HO	87:1	3.5mm/1ft
N	160:1	2mm/1ft
Z	220:1	1.5mm/1ft

STANDARD GAUGE COMPARISON

SHOWN FULL SIZE

6.5 Z
9.5 N
16.5mm HO/OO
32mm O
45mm 1
Track gauge

9 It is interesting to note the difference between the height of the OO and HO gauge locomotives, which share the same 16.5mm track gauge. This rather suggests that in the interests of realism the two gauges should not be mixed.

is O gauge, thus opening up a whole new world of realism. Factors which militate against O and 1 gauges are cost and space – but on the latter point these gauges are eminently suitable for outdoor railways.

N, OO and O gauges have corresponding narrow gauge counterparts, each making use of the next size down in standard gauge; and suitable locomotives and rolling stock are available for specialists in this field. Finally, the largest of all scales is SM-32 at 16mm to 1ft, which, as it is classified as narrow gauge, makes use of O gauge trackwork.

Period layouts

Many modellers turn to actual sections of real railways, past or present, for inspiration in the design of their layouts. It may be that the appeal of a particular configuration of track or the appearance of a group of railway buildings is something they feel worthy of being incorporated in their scheme. Others may wish to reproduce faithfully every small detail of a specific branch line which has some special significance for them. These modellers will need to do careful research before making a start on the planning stage of their layouts. If the railway is still in existence, photographs taken on site will be of great value. If not, the

local library or history group is a good starting point for a source of suitable material. The relevant parts of the track, station platforms and buildings must be carefully drawn out, paying particular attention to size and scale. If dimensions are not available on the material obtained, it is helpful to remember that four brick courses are about 12in (300mm) high, and a doorway is roughly 6ft 9in (2060mm) high. The true atmosphere of the scene will begin to develop when the smallest details are modelled: the planked crossing over the tracks between the platforms, the ivy growing over the back of the signal cabin or the broken awning on the newsagent's stand.

Whether you decide to model an actual railway or not, it is very important that you study small details for inclusion on your layout. Next time you make a railway journey, or are near a railway, make notes and sketches to help you remember – observation is of far greater value than memory or imagination. Realism grows with the addition of each item: the white-painted trackside gradient signs, the types of fencing used, the smoke stains on the footbridge over the tracks and so on. Colour photographs are an excellent means of recording the details, enabling you to add the finishing touches that make the difference between a mediocre and a first class layout.

2 Baseboards and trackwork

Baseboard supporting system

Having selected the location for your layout, chosen the gauge and planned it in some detail, the time has come to make a start on construction. You will need a firm foundation for the layout, a structure strong enough to take your own weight, for inevitably you will climb on to the baseboard at some stage of the track-laying procedure. Visitors, too, will never be entirely dissuaded from leaning on the completed model, and the rigours of construction itself all point to the necessity of a stout supporting system.

10 This exploded view shows the construction of framing for a standard 4ft × 2ft (1200mm × 600mm) baseboard unit. All timber is 2in × 1in (50mm × 25mm) spaced at 12in (300mm) centres both ways. All joints, whether half-lapped or butted, are glued and screwed.

The frame for the baseboard should be constructed of 2in × 1in (50mm × 25mm) prepared (planed) timber bearers, arranged so that the minimum span in either direction is 12in (300mm). The main runs of timber should be half-lap jointed at intersections as shown in figure 10, while the bracing members need only be butt-joined, glued and screwed. You will need to cut down the 8ft × 4ft (2400mm × 1200mm) sheets of baseboard material to a size that can easily be handled, and as stated in Chapter 1 the optimum size is 4ft × 2ft (1200mm × 600mm). This is the size to which the frames will be constructed, unless you are building a permanent layout where you might consider larger sizes appropriate.

Another rather more expensive method of constructing baseboards is to use flush doors.

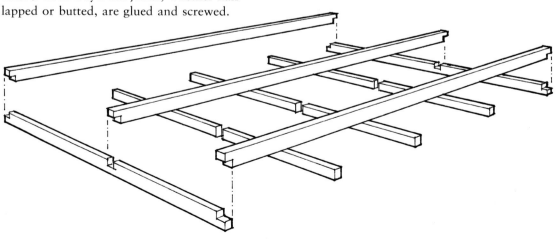

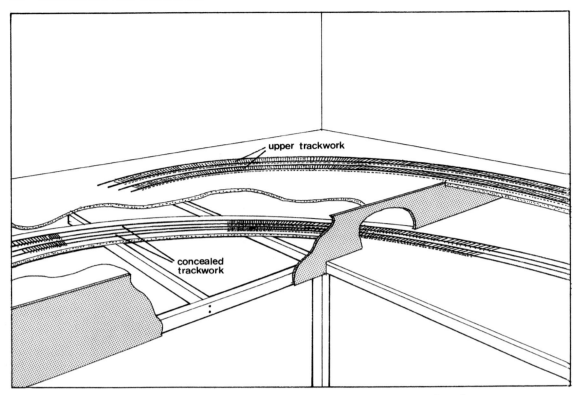

11 The concealed trackwork at the lower level is laid on a narrow width of baseboard supported on framing, allowing access to trains from below.

These are rigid, and those built with an egg-crate core are light and strong. However, the plywood or hardboard finish on these doors is not really suitable for track fixing, and it is recommended that fibreboard sheeting be fixed over the upper surface. You must also bear in mind the problems involved in transporting a unit as large as a door.

If you have designed a multi-level layout, you will have to consider at this stage how you will gain access to trains travelling on concealed levels. The best method of doing this is to use continuous baseboards only at the upper levels of the layout, the hidden trackwork being fixed to narrow strips of baseboard material cut to the configuration of the track (see figure 11). This allows access

from below to correct derailments or to carry out track cleaning.

The reverse of this is quite commonly encountered, and consists of a solid baseboard at the lowest level with a number of ramps or gradients rising and falling in the course of the railway. This has the advantage of overcoming the monotony of tracks laid all at one level, and used in conjunction with rolling scenery can be most effective. You may consider 'dropping' sections of the baseboard to allow for major changes in the landscape, such as valleys or ravines. This gives the opportunity of building a bridge or a viaduct as well as the possibility of a river in the valley, all greatly adding to the interest of the model (see figure 12).

If you are constructing a permanent layout, the supporting framework may now be fixed in position. You may be able to attach the frames to the walls of your model room, or to convenient roof timbers of your loft, with legs

12 A section of the baseboard has been dropped to form a valley. The line passes over a bridge which spans the river below.

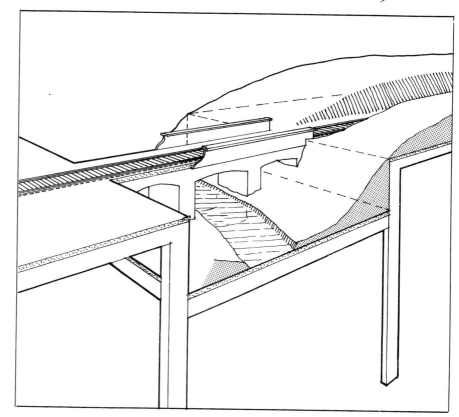

13 Some of the framing members have been extended to allow the back of the baseboard unit to be screwed to the rafters. The front is carried on legs at 4ft (1200mm) centres. Note that the flooring has only been laid where essential, and also that the fibreglass insulation has been carried right down to the bottom of the loft space.

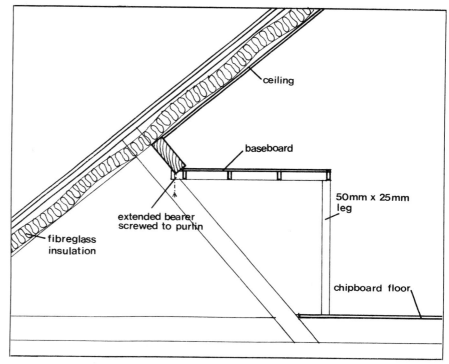

ceiling

baseboard

50mm x 25mm leg

extended bearer screwed to purlin

fibreglass insulation

chipboard floor

along the front edge only, as shown in figure 13. For foldaway or portable layouts the frames can be supported on trestles, folding legs, or even on a table. In the latter case small squares of leatherette or some similar material should be glued at intervals to the underside of the framing to protect the table and prevent the baseboard from sliding.

Baseboards

There are a limited number of materials from which you should choose your baseboards if problems are to be avoided in laying the trackwork. Both plywood and hardboard are unsuitable as they are far too hard for the insertion of track pins, and are never quite level. It is essential to have a level surface as a turnout fitted over a bump in the baseboard causes endless difficulties.

Modellers agree that the best baseboards are constructed using $\frac{1}{2}$in (12mm) medium-hard fibreboard, such as Sundeala. This fibreboard has a perfectly flat surface, an ideal density for track fixing and can be cut cleanly and easily. It is also not too heavy, which makes it particularly suitable for portable layouts. If your local timber merchant does not keep this material in stock, he will probably be prepared to order a few sheets for you. There is also the advantage that the material can be supplied in sheets ready cut to 4ft × 2ft (1200mm × 600mm) instead of the more usual 8ft × 4ft (2400mm × 1200mm).

An alternative is $\frac{1}{2}$in (12mm) insulation board, but although it is cheap and light this material has a very low density. Simply fixing track with long track pins is probably not enough to secure it rigidly, and you will have to resort to other means to ensure that the track does not move. You may also have to make use of additional bracing in the supporting frames, in which case you might as well have invested in the proper material in the first place.

Another material commonly used is $\frac{1}{2}$in (12mm) chipboard, probably because it is roughly one-third of the cost of Sundeala board. However, if you do decide to use this material, bear in mind its far greater weight and the effects that this might have on handling and cutting. It is also essential that once the baseboard has been laid you go over it very carefully with a long metal straight-edge or builder's level in order to determine where the bumps occur. These can then be removed with a sanding disc or a plane. It may sound like an unnecessary amount of hard labour, but if it is not done now, there will be no opportunity later, and you will certainly regret the omission.

Joining baseboards

As a single 4ft × 2ft (1200mm × 600mm) baseboard panel is unlikely to be the limit of your ambitions, you will have to provide a means of linking panels so that the complete layout can be assembled without too much difficulty. This must be done in such a way that the panels are securely and accurately joined, with no possibility of movement. This can be achieved by screwing to the sides of the completed panels 2in (50mm) hinges, across the panel joints. The hinge pin must be removed and replaced with a stout length of wire of the same gauge, and the wire bent to a convenient shape to facilitate withdrawal (see figure 14).

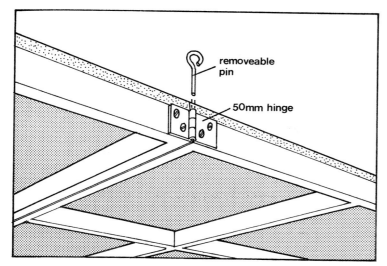

14 Joining baseboard units. The hinge is screwed across the joint, and the pin is replaced with a piece of wire of the same gauge.

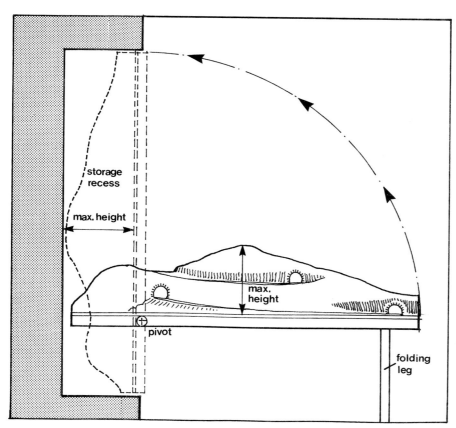

15 A foldaway layout. Ensure that the full height of the landscaping can be accommodated in the recess.

Folding layouts

The method you use to allow your layout to be folded away when not in use will depend on the particular location you have chosen for it. Nevertheless, some of the principles of folding apply in all cases, perhaps the most important being that you must make provision for the accommodation of the landscaping. For this reason it is necessary to consider the height of all built-up areas before proceeding too far with the baseboard construction (see figure 15).

Gradients

A gradient of about 1:70 is about the steepest on a real railway system, but on model layouts space will often decree steeper inclines. Drive wheels on locomotives fitted with rubber or plastic tyres will cope with very heavy gradients, but in the interests of realism 1:30 is the maximum you should consider. The purpose of a gradient on a model layout is often to allow one track to pass over another, and the absolute minimum clearance for this is 2½in (63.5mm) (see figure 16). To this must be added the thickness of the material from which the flyover is constructed, perhaps ½in (12mm) so that it can be seen that to reach the required height of 3in (76mm), the length of the gradient will need to be a minimum of 2.28m, about 7½ft.

In forming the gradient from a strip of baseboard material the difficult part is to curve the lower end evenly to meet the level baseboard. The easiest way of doing this is to make two parallel cuts in the baseboard with a jigsaw or keyhole saw, and then to raise this strip by means of blocks to the desired slope (see figure 17). Both fibreboard and chipboard are sufficiently flexible for this to be done. To make the corresponding gentle curve at the

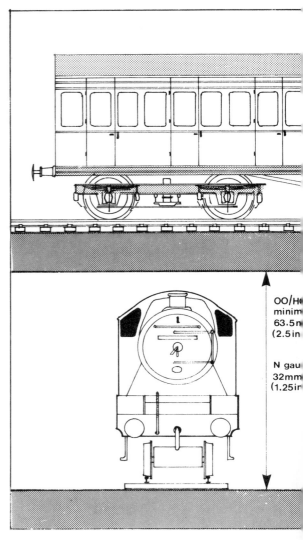

16 Minimum clearance for a flyover crossing.

top of the gradient, use a separate strip of baseboard material cut to the same width as the first. Make a number of sawcuts about 1in (25mm) apart on the underside, almost through the thickness of the material. This will enable you to bend the board to the required curve, and the shape can be held by using a few blocks of scrap timber glued and screwed below (see figure 18).

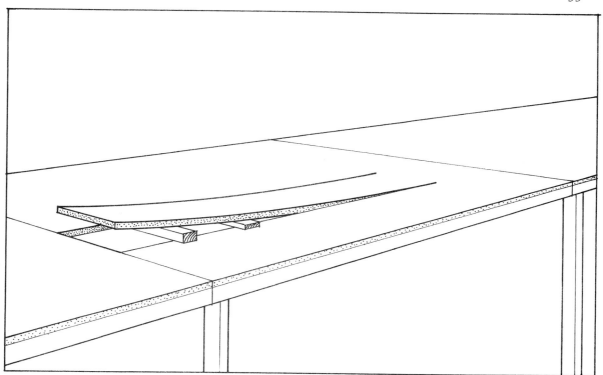

17 The lower end of a gradient. Two parallel sawcuts are made in the baseboard and the trackway wedged to the required slope by means of scrap blocks of wood.

18 (*Below*) The upper end of a gradient. The sawcuts on the underside of the trackway make it easier to bend the material to conform to the required shape. The supporting blocks are glued and screwed for permanence.

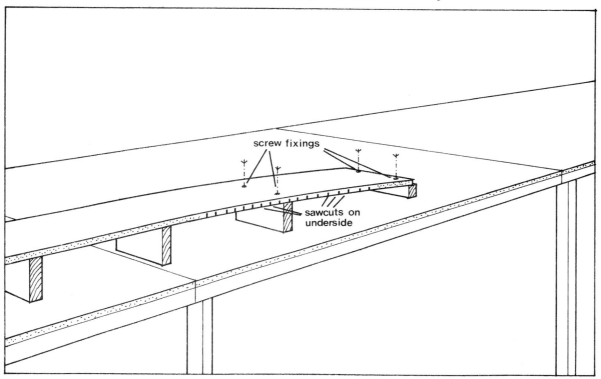

Backscene panel

It is important to avoid the impression that the completed scenic layout stops abruptly at the back of the baseboard. An illusion of depth can be created by making the scenery appear to recede into the distance, and for this the technique of perspective will need to be employed. Whether this is achieved by your own artistic efforts or by the application of one of the colour-printed backdrops is unimportant at this stage; what now has to be done is to make suitable provision for it. A continuous panel of hardboard at least 1ft (300mm) high must be attached to the back of each of the baseboard sections or, in the case of a permanent layout, fixed to the wall behind. It will be necessary to make this removable so that the backscene can be conveniently applied, as well as for the easier handling of portable layouts.

Type of track

The baseboards should now be ready for you to set out the exact location of all the trackwork. You must, however, first decide upon the type of track you are going to install:

- *Set track:* this is easy to lay, and to take up and relay, but the sudden transition from curved to straight track lacks realism;
- *Flexible track:* this overcomes the criticism of set track, but requires greater care in laying accurately. A mixture of compatible types of track from the same manufacturer is possible;
- *Hand built:* this might be considered where a complex set of turnouts and crossings is being built as an exact replica of a real section of railway. The cost of components has now risen to the point where it is no longer more economical to use than ready-made trackwork.

Type of ballast

The other decision you will need to make before marking out the lines of track concerns the type of ballast you intend to use. You can fix the track directly to the baseboard and build up the ballast around it afterwards, or you can use one of the flexible foam ballast underlays, such as the one marketed by Peco, which has the impression of track moulded into it. Your choice will depend on whether you want smooth, silent running, or the rather noisy, but not unrealistic, sound of trains on hard ballast, complete with wheel-clicks over rail joints. The reason for making this decision now is that setting-out lines need to be positioned accordingly. In the case of foam underlay, the setting-out line will represent the inner edge of the foam; while with no underlay the inner edge of the sleepers will follow this line.

Another very realistic method is to lay the track on scraps of vinyl flooring (such as the kind often laid in kitchens), which flooring specialists may be prepared to give you free of charge. This material raises the track fractionally above baseboard level, and is well worth the extra effort entailed. The common thicknesses of 3mm and 4mm (about $\frac{1}{8}$in) give just about the right amount of elevation. The vinyl is cut roughly to size and fixed down at the same time as the track, afterwards being cut accurately to a line just outside the edge of the sleepers.

Setting out the trackwork

You will need a straight edge or a narrow strip of carefully-cut hardboard about 4ft (1200mm) long for marking the straight runs of track, and a felt-tip pen. Curves can be set out by using the same hardboard strip. Drill in the strip a number of small holes to give a

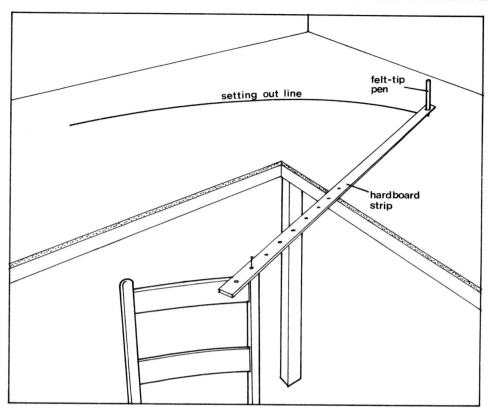

setting out line

felt-tip pen

hardboard strip

19 The hardboard strip, which can also be used as a straightedge, is here being used to scribe a large radius setting-out line.

range of radii, and a larger hole at one end into which the pen can be pushed. Temporarily drive a panel pin into the baseboard at the appropriate point to give the radius centre required, and scribe off the curve. If the centre of the curve occurs off the baseboard, use the back of a chair as a fixing point. Try to give a gradual transition from curved to straight runs in the way prototype track is laid. Remember that you are setting out the inner edge of the sleepers or foam underlay, not the centre of the track.

Where turnouts occur, particular care must be taken if problems are to be avoided at a later stage. The tracks on either side must be cut with the rail ends *exactly* parallel to the sleepers – any projections will prevent a smooth transition from track to turnout. Peco produces sheets of full-sized plans of all their *Streamline* turnouts and crossings, and these can be cut out and taped to the baseboard for accurate setting out.

Most manufacturers give the standard dimension between the centres of parallel tracks for OO/HO gauge as $2\frac{5}{8}$in (67mm). It is, however, difficult to be specific about this measurement. In prototype steam railways the expression 'six-foot way' was coined as the supposed dimension between the inner rails of two parallel tracks. However, this tended to vary considerably – on curves, and where obstructions occurred between tracks, for instance – and the term came to refer simply to the space between tracks, regardless of the actual measurement. On model layouts to OO/HO gauge, where, to scale, the track is undersized and the overhang on locomotives and rolling stock is rather more than prototype, it is not possible to space the trackwork so closely. It is advisable, then, to adhere to the recommended 2⅝in (67mm) standard unless you have very good reason to do otherwise.

Laying the track

In selecting your track, you must decide whether you want to use treated steel rail or the more expensive solid nickel silver. The latter has the distinct advantage, which more than compensates for the extra cost, that there is no coating to wear off, and occasional cleaning is all that is needed to maintain good electrical contact. You can also choose between wooden sleepers for older types of installation and modern precast concrete sleepers. (Peco *Streamline* trackwork has been designed and manufactured to fine scale standards, and is generally acknowledged to be the most realistic ready-made track available.)

Begin with a straight run of track, using a full 36in (1m) length of flexible track. Cut away the plastic chairs that attach the rails to the sleepers at both ends of the track, to allow the insertion of rail joiners. Lay the track on the baseboard with the edge of the sleepers (or the edge of the underlay) precisely against the setting-out line, and drive a trackpin through the second sleeper. (The first sleeper is no longer attached to the track.) Do not drive any of the pins fully home until all the tracklaying has been completed, or you may damage the track in trying to lift and relocate it. Use a pin punch with a flat head and do not hammer directly on to the pins, or you will damage the back. Use five or six pins to secure this one length of track, finishing with a pin through the penultimate sleeper as before.

Now push a pair of rail joiners on to the ends of the track already fixed, and slide the next section of track up to it so that a firm connection is made. Never try to join the sections in mid-air, for the joiners will not fit tightly and may cause poor electrical connection. Remember to insert nylon isolating rail joiners where required as you proceed. If in doubt about the final circuitry of your layout, use more isolating joiners, as it is easier to reconnect the sections than to disconnect them. Before pinning the next section of track to the baseboard, see that the spacing of sleepers across the joint is constant – you may have to ease some of the sleepers along a little to achieve this. Sometimes it is necessary to insert a spare sleeper under joints in order to achieve even sleeper spacing.

Curves

As the track is made to follow a curved setting-out line, you will see that the inner rail becomes longer than the outer. This extra length must be cut away to the line of the sleepers, which automatically follow the radius line. A junior hacksaw can be used for this; hold it up against a wooden block that has been notched to fit over the rails so that the track can be held firmly. You may find it easier to make all your cutting strokes in one direction, as the blade tends to jam if used with a to-and-fro motion (see figure 21). An alternative and easier method is to use a small corundum wheel in a miniature electric drill (such as the one marketed by *Minicraft*). This device is a worthwhile investment, and you will later find it invaluable in making cuts to isolate trackwork electrically. It is virtually impossible to insert isolating joiners into rails after they have been laid.

As each pin is tapped in, check by sighting along the rails that there are no wiggles and that the straight or curved tracks run truly. However accurate your setting out has been, the smallest deviation – even by the thickness of the setting-out line itself – will show up unless great care is taken.

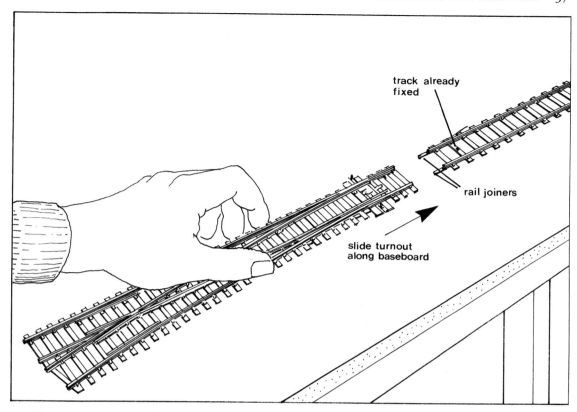

track already
fixed

rail joiners

slide turnout
along baseboard

20 The correct way to make a joint in trackwork. The next section of track, or a turnout, should be slid along the baseboard to meet the rail joiners attached to the track already laid. Never attempt to make the joint by holding both sections of track in mid-air.

21 Cutting trackwork. The wood block, which has two parallel grooves on the underside, fits over the track. This allows firm pressure on the sleepers while the junior hacksaw is being used.

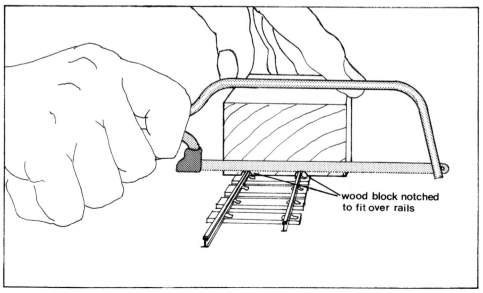

wood block notched
to fit over rails

Turnouts

These require especially careful treatment. You will already have ensured that the baseboard is perfectly true and level. The next step is to slide the facing end of the turnout up to the rail joiners fixed to the last section of track to check that the rails have been cut to the correct length. Then carefully remove the turnout and temporarily fit a turnout motor (if required) to the underside in accordance with the leaflet provided by the manufacturers. By sighting down through the sleepers you will be able to determine the exact amount of space required to fit the motor into the baseboard. Make small marks on the sleepers to fix these dimensions, then remove the motor and replace the turnout on the baseboard in position so that the marks can be transferred to the baseboard. Allow the smallest possible amount of clearance – no more than one or two millimetres – and cut out the piece of baseboard using a keyhole saw. Now fit the motor permanently to the turnout, giving the fixing lugs a 45° twist with a pair of pliers, and set the turnout in position on the baseboard. You will find it convenient to solder the connecting wires to the motor

before inserting it into place. Details of how to do this are given on page 62.

An alternative method of connecting the tie bar of the turnout to the drive motor can be used, which avoids having to cut a hole in the baseboard. An extension pin and connecting sleeve is provided with each motor, and this passes through a small hole drilled in the baseboard (the motor is simply fastened to the underside of the baseboard by means of screws and washers). As before, accurate positioning is vital.

It will only be necessary to carry out the positioning exercise once because, when you have determined the location of the opening for one motor in relation to the turnout sleepers, marking off openings for subsequent motors is quite straightforward.

It is also possible to fit the drive motor on top of the baseboard adjacent to the tie bar. This is sometimes necessary where a supporting batten occurs immediately below the turnout. The motor can subsequently be disguised under a plate-layer's hut or similar trackside building.

Fixing holes are generally marked on turnout sleepers, but you should try to use the minimum number of pins needed to make the

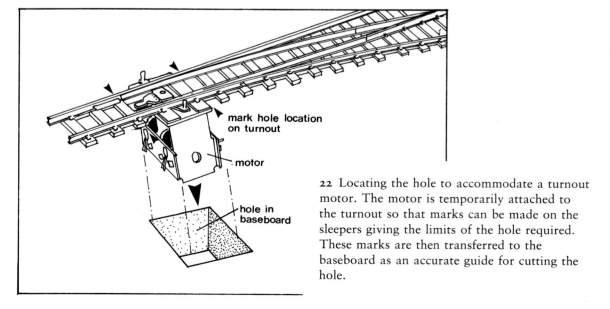

mark hole location on turnout

motor

hole in baseboard

22 Locating the hole to accommodate a turnout motor. The motor is temporarily attached to the turnout so that marks can be made on the sleepers giving the limits of the hole required. These marks are then transferred to the baseboard as an accurate guide for cutting the hole.

turnout lie flat. Once again, these should not be fully driven home, and leaving the pin-heads projecting about a millimetre helps to ensure that the turnout is not twisted. If the *frog* or crossing is bent upwards by the tiniest amount, derailments will inevitably occur.

Once you are completely satisfied that the requirements for the correct laying of a turnout have been met, you can proceed with the trackwork on the 'out' side of the turnout. When a length of track has been laid to each

of the turnout arms, you can test its operation by pushing a carriage over it, trying the switch in either direction.

Portable layouts

When laying trackwork across the joints in a series of baseboard panels, the main difficulty is devising a system of aligning the rails accurately on subsequent occasions. Even when the method described on page 30 is used to secure the panels, a millimetre discrepancy in track alignment will cause derailments. Lay the trackwork in the usual manner, with the panels securely joined, but insert the last track-fixing pin about 6in (150mm) on either side of the joint, so that

23 Joining trackwork across two portable baseboard units. The last track pin is inserted about 5in (150mm) from the join on either side to allow some flexibility. Rail joiners provide the alignment, and electrical continuity is guaranteed by the use of the connector below the baseboard.

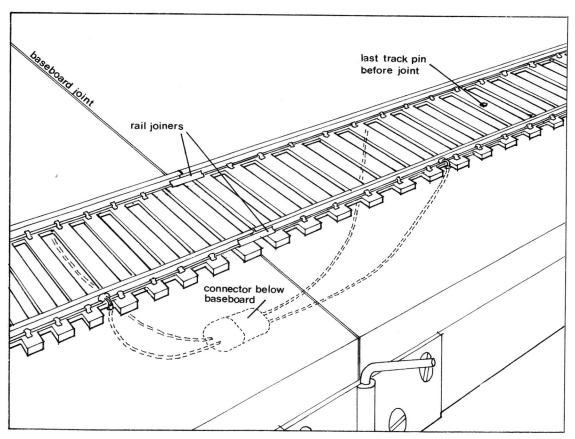

baseboard joint

last track pin
before joint

rail joiners

connector below
baseboard

there is a degree of play in the track. Cut through the rails on the line of the joint, using a corundum wheel or the block method shown in figure 21. Rail joiners pushed fully on to one of the two pairs of rails to be joined can be slid out to align the track when you assemble the layout, using a pair of long-nosed pliers to pinch them tightly in place. This, however, does not guarantee the conductivity of the joint, and you will need to solder a length of multistrand wire to *the outside* of each of the four rails. These wires are taken below the baseboard through small holes drilled between the sleeper ends, and can be connected by soldering, twisting together or by means of small plugs and sockets (see figure 23).

Ballasting the track

Many modellers prefer to carry out ballasting as the next stage of the construction work, but this seems to offer no particular benefit. It is important that you carry out all the wiring before laying the ballast, to avoid touching up where holes have been drilled. You should also set in place at the very least the walls of station platforms, to avoid having to remove excess ballast later on. There may be other encroachments close to the track, and so on balance it would seem preferable to leave ballasting until the model is much further advanced.

The first thing to do is to apply rust to the track. Manufacturers do not appear to have appreciated that shiny rail sides do much to detract from authenticity, and all good modellers carry out this exercise as a matter of course. The rust-coloured paint, such as Humbrol *Track Colour*, can be applied using a small brush, or you can spray the complete

24 The station platform walls should be in position before ballasting is begun.

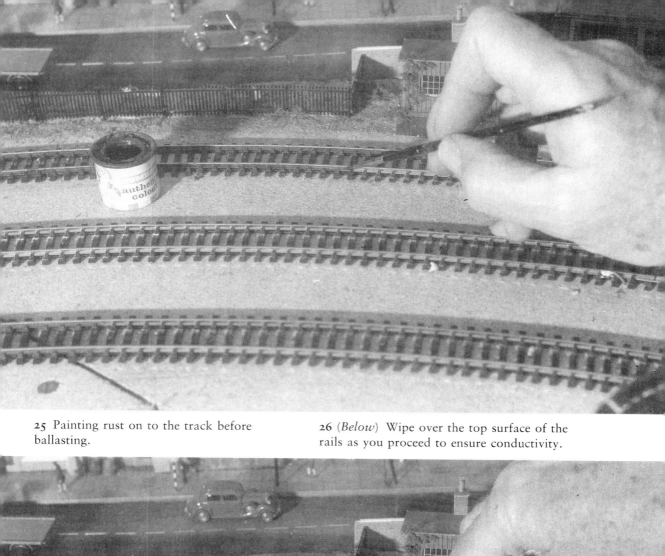

25 Painting rust on to the track before ballasting.

26 (*Below*) Wipe over the top surface of the rails as you proceed to ensure conductivity.

27 Use a teaspoon to apply the resin/ballast mixture to the track.

28 (*Below*) Carefully brush the mixture into position, ensuring that the tops of the sleepers are not covered.

29 Let us spray. . . .

ballasted track with a car aerosol primer. Spraying will require some masking to the surroundings, and this can be done by laying newspaper on either side of the track up to the line of the ballast. Track, ballast and sleepers end up the same authentic, dull, red-brown colour. Whichever method you use, remember it is vital to wipe clean the top and inside edge of the rails as you proceed in order to maintain electrical contact. Similarly, no paint must be applied to the inside of turnout blades, or to the adjoining stock rails.

Quite realistic ballast is available as fine cork granules, but the most effective material is a scaled-down version of real ballast, made from granite chippings. The authentic appearance of the latter makes the extra expense well worth while. Mix in a dry jam-jar a quantity of ballast with waterproof wood glue such as Cascamite in the proportion of two parts of ballast to one of the powdered resin glue. Rotate and shake the closed jar well until the contents are thoroughly mixed, then apply the mix to the track with a teaspoon. Using a small, stiff brush (such as the one used by artists for oil painting) coax the mixture into place so that it is level with, but not covering, the sleepers. The ballast should extend a little way beyond the sleepers on either side. When you have satisfactorily completed a metre or so of several parallel tracks, fill a pint-sized hand-operated greenhouse spray with water and a teaspoonful of washing-up liquid. Set the nozzle to a fine mist and spray the liquid over the ballasted track. The washing-up liquid acts as a wetting agent, and the Cascamite glue is activated by the water. After 24 hours the ballast will have set rock hard, and all that remains to be done is to polish the upper edge of the rails to remove any glue, and to vacuum up any chippings which have escaped the setting process.

Great care must be taken in laying this type of ballast around turnouts, as the granules can easily interfere with their smooth operation. Ensure that no ballast has become entrapped between the blades, around the frog, or on top of the chairs, and that all ballast is permanently fixed in position. Check the turnout by pushing a wagon over it in both directions before the ballast mixture has finally set.

Laying foam ballast

Foam underlay is available in 16ft (5m) lengths. The track is laid into the moulded outline in the foam, which is then cut into track lengths. A smear of PVA glue is applied to the underside of the foam, and the section of track and foam set in position on the baseboard. Press down firmly, and allow the glue to ooze through the foam sufficiently to contact the underside of the sleepers. If necessary, track pins can be used temporarily to hold the assembly in place, but these are really only required on curves. It is recommended that the minimum number of pins be used because of the possibility of distorting the track level; the assembly will lie perfectly flat without pins.

3 Control systems

For adequate and realistic control of your layout you will need a minimum of two independent controllers of at least 1 amp rating each, perhaps with a facility for future expansion. There are a number of such units available from model railway suppliers, each with its own particular merits. It is useful to have transformer tappings for 16v AC and 12v DC uncontrolled outlets. The 16v AC supply is used for operating solenoids (such as those on turnout motors), and the 12v DC for lighting and signalling circuits. Some controllers provide switching for high and low resistance motors, and full or half-wave pulse-power control, the latter for improved slow-running speeds. There should be an automatic self-setting overload cutout to protect the locomotives and the unit. Closed loop feedback controllers compensate automatically for gradients and give particularly smooth running, and are a worthwhile investment.

In operating model layouts, a common

30 A typical transformer controller with dual regulators. (*Courtesy of Gaugemaster*)

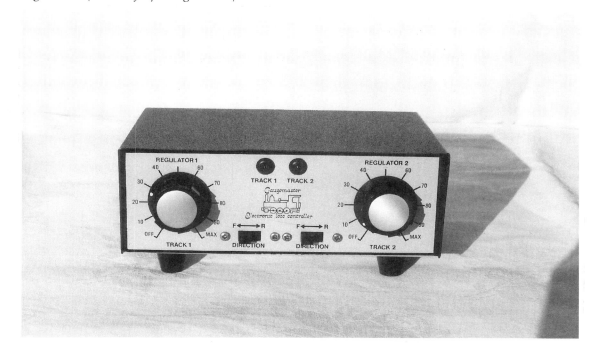

31 The comprehensive control panel of the 7mm gauge model railway on display at the National Railway Museum in York. (*Courtesy of the National Railway Museum*)

mistake is to run the trains at unrealistically high speeds. It is all very well if the section of the track represents the line carrying the *Flying Scotsman*, but this is the exception rather than the rule. More often you will be dealing with goods trains travelling at speeds of 30mph or less, and slow passenger trains on frequent stopping routes. To get a good idea of the speed represented by your model, a section of track 3ft (900mm) long should be marked off with two pieces of masking tape beside the line. An OO gauge train travelling at a scale speed of 30mph will take a full five seconds to pass these two markers – which may seem surprisingly slow. Even at 60mph it will still take two and a half seconds. This is a

useful exercise and a lesson to curb the tendency to turn the control knob to full speed. Realistic train speeds are just as important on the layout as realism in the modelling of the scenery and buildings.

Of course, clean track and clean locomotive pickup wheels are essential to achieve smooth, slow running, and regular maintenance must not be neglected. If the layout has not been used for some time, wipe over the trackwork with a piece of cloth moistened with methylated spirits to remove accumulated grime. The same means will clean pickup wheels on locomotives or tenders. Do not attempt to rotate driving wheels by hand, or the gears will be damaged. Touch the wheels to the track momentarily with the controller set to slow speed to obtain a partial turn, thus making the next dirty segments of the wheels accessible.

Computer control

With the arrival of the computer age it was perhaps inevitable that the microchip would find its way into the field of model railways. An ingenious system is available as an alternative to the conventional arrangement of isolated blocks of track, each with independent controls. The microchip dispenses with wiring to each section, turnout motors and signal lights, and adds some previously impossible elements of train control.

A system known as *Zero 1* was introduced in 1979 by Hornby Hobbies, consisting of a master control unit connected by a single pair of wires to the trackwork. The whole track carried a steady 18vAC and eliminated all isolators. Up to 16 locomotives could be controlled independently by punching out a unique code on the control unit, the code being recognised by a module installed in each locomotive. This module translated requirements regarding speed and direction, as well as rectifying the current, and allowed the locomotive to move accordingly. Further modules, each recognising a separate code, could be installed to operate turnout motors and signal lights. A mimic 'signal box' display system was introduced in 1981, but because of poor sales was subsequently discontinued. Later the main control unit itself was withdrawn, presumably for similar reasons. Currently, only slave units that operate from the master unit are available, together with locomotive modules. It seems that insurmountable problems beset the scheme, including the need to keep the trackwork scrupulously clean in order to avoid control codes being misinterpreted by the modules.

Developments to this type of system have been made by other model railway specialists, such as Fleischmann and Märklin, but the problem is the cost of this equipment, probably considerably beyond the means of the average enthusiast. It may be, too, that modellers are not eager to dispense with the absorbing process of installing control systems for their layouts, and are reluctant to let the computer take over yet another aspect of their lives.

Serious railway modellers, such as those who provide articles for magazines dealing with the subject, frequently concentrate their efforts on a realistic layout that represents an actual or imagined section of a railway at a definite period of time. The pleasure in their hobby is derived partly from the construction of the layout, the engines and rolling stock, and partly from the careful and accurate operation of trains to a real or at least probable schedule: the occasional passage of an express to the big city, the arrival of the empty wagons for loading at the local factory, the suburban passenger train steaming into platform 2, and so on. Each movement is carried out with meticulous attention to detail, down to the correct headcodes on the diesels, the livery of the porters standing on the platform and the name of the newspaper advertised on the hoarding – all the result of a great deal of patient research. The assembly of trains is carried out discreetly behind a screen in a fiddle yard so that out-of-scale human hands need not appear over the backdrop.

To these enthusiasts, the idea of computer control or any form of automation may well be an anathema. Yet for the enthusiast who spends precious evenings shut away in his loft or garage building up his model railway project, there may well be some scope for the introduction of automatic control. Not being involved with a club, he may confine his sharing to showing off proudly his efforts to occasional visitors, or discussing some aspect of the layout with another lone enthusiast. In his case, it may be desirable to have part of the system running automatically, retaining another section for manual control of shunting and other localized operations. This will certainly give a busy overall impression and bring the layout to life. Indeed, for all those who are intrigued with the apparent magic of automation, much pleasure is to be gained from the total or partial use of this type of system. If the cost of proprietary makes of automatic equipment is too daunting, then the following pages offer a do-it-yourself means of achieving the result at a modest cost, together with the satisfaction always associated with making something from a few bits and pieces.

Inertia simulation

Incorporating inertia simulation in the control circuit adds a new dimension to the operation of model trains. The system works by introducing the effect on the locomotive of having to overcome the inertia of a heavy load of wagons in pulling away or in braking. Before setting the train in motion, one control is adjusted to represent this inertia, and another the braking power of the train. For example, a diesel electric unit on its own would be able to move away and brake rapidly, while a steam engine pulling 20 coal wagons would obviously take some time to reach the desired running speed, and even with brakes applied hard would slow down gradually. A regulator control is thus moved, say, to half power and after a moment or two the train begins to move away, slowly gathering speed as the regulator is opened further. When running speed has been achieved, close the regulator and the train will continue to coast, gradually losing speed. If the brake is engaged the train will slow down and eventually stop after some considerable distance in a most realistic fashion. Some skill is required in controlling the train using this method, and there is great satisfaction in stopping a passenger train so that the carriages are positioned correctly in relation to the station platform.

There are several simulator units available which function adequately, but savings can be made by constructing the simulator described here. It can be incorporated in the main control panel, and switched in and out of circuit as required.

This circuit (figure 33) originally appeared in the *Railway Modeller* magazine some years ago in an article by N. M. Narracott. It has

32 A dual simulator unit for panel mounting. The simulator effect can be switched out if required, in which case the regulator operates in the normal way. (*Courtesy of Gaugemaster*)

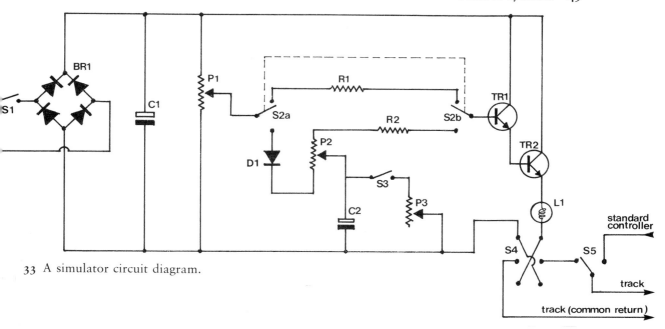

33 A simulator circuit diagram.

been slightly modified to control the power supply from the main controller, and a facility added to introduce simulation only when needed.

The components are as follows:

S1	SP on/off switch
S2	DPDT switch
S3	press-to-make pushbutton
S4	DPDT switch
S5	2-way switch (SPDT)
R1	1kΩ resistor
R2	5.6kΩ resistor
D1	IN4001 silicon diode
TR1	BC107
TR2	2N3055 (NPN)
C1	50μ F electrolytic capacitor 25v
C2	500μ F electrolytic capacitor 25v
P1	10kΩ linear potentiometer
P2	1kΩ linear potentiometer
P3	1kΩ linear potentiometer
BR1	12v bridge rectifier (2amp)

Construction (see figure 34)

Drill the holes required for the fascia-mounted components, remembering the locking holes for the nibs on the potentiometers. Cut a piece of aluminium sheeting to carry the main electronic components, and another smaller piece for the heat sink. This is an essential part of this circuit, as the power transistor generates enough heat to destroy itself should this heat not be dissipated. Fold the larger piece as shown after cutting a hole for potentiometer P1, and bolt on two six-way tag strips. The aluminium panel may now be fitted to the back of the fascia panel, using P1 to secure it. Fix in position the remaining fascia-mounted components. The capacitors, diode, resistors and transistors may now be soldered in and the remaining wiring carried out. A good way to check your progress is to make a tracing of the circuit diagram, or obtain a photocopy, and mark off each component and length of wiring as you proceed, to ensure that no connections are omitted. Take particular care when soldering

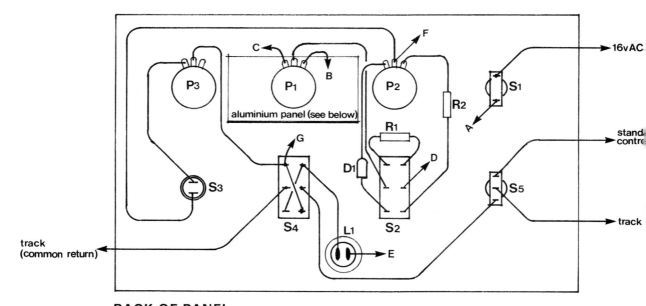

34 Layout of components for the simulator circuit shown in figure 33.

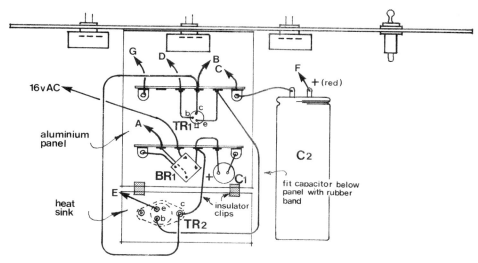

TOP VIEW OF OPPOSITE LAYOUT

in the transistors: hold the connnecting wires in a pair of needle-nosed pliers as a heat shunt, and use only enough heat to melt the solder. After fitting TR2 to the heat sink, clip it to the back of the aluminium panel with two small insulator blocks, which can be made from a piece of plastic. (Nylon curtain-track supports were used on the prototype.) Slot the insulators between the heat sink and aluminium panel and fix with a dab of epoxy resin glue.

It is important that the 12VDC power supply for this device comes from an independent source. Do not use the 16VDC outlet on your controller if you are using the common return system, or interference will occur. Ideally use a separate transformer, which can be switched into circuit when the inertia system is being used.

Automatic block control

The object of block control is to prevent trains travelling at different speeds in the same direction and on the same track from running into one another. Several manufacturers market equipment for block control, but you might like to try making your own, which is considerably cheaper.

The particular item of equipment that makes block control possible is a *latching relay* or, alternatively, a *double-throw relay*. Most relays work on the principle that when an electromagnet is energized a set of contacts are made, which are broken when the current is cut off. With latching relays, however, two electromagnets are employed and changeover contacts are provided.

The other device needed is a *reed switch*, which consists of two thin steel contacts fixed slightly apart in a glass tube from which the air has been withdrawn. When a magnet is passed over the switch the steel contacts are drawn together momentarily, allowing a current to pass.

The principle of block control can be

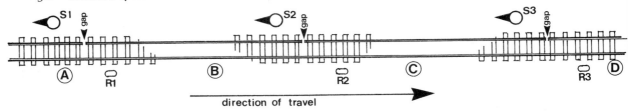

35

understood by referring to figure 35. A train travelling on section A will pass a green light displayed on signal S1, and enter section B. Signal S2 will also be green, and the train will enter section C. As a magnet attached to the underside of some part of the train passes over reed switch R2, one electromagnet of the latching relay is momentarily energized and a new set of contacts made. These change signal S1 to red and cut off the power supply to section B. This prevents another train on section A from entering section B, and it will wait at the red light S1. When the first train enters section D, the operation of the reed switch R3 will cause the second electromagnet of the latching relay to be energized. The changeover switch will alter signal S1 to green and restore power to section B. The two trains will proceed, always maintaining at least one full section of track between them.

For two trains running on a block controlled circuit it is necessary to have at least *five* isolated sections (or *blocks*) in the system. Figure 36 shows two trains on a loop with only four blocks. The train on section A will have cut off the power to section D, and the second train on section C will have cut off the power to section B. Neither train will be able to proceed on to the next section of track. However, in figure 37, where five blocks are provided, the train on section A is able to proceed on to section B, thus restoring power to section E and enabling the train on section D to proceed. There is no limit to the number of blocks which may be included in a loop layout, provided that there are always three

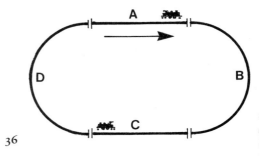

36

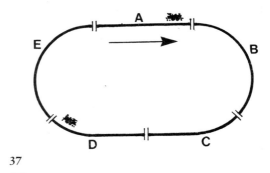

37

more blocks than the number of trains you intend to run at once; that is, six blocks for three trains, seven for four trains and so on.

Figure 38 shows a typical latching relay, and figure 39 two such relays mounted on a home-made printed circuit board. It is, of course, quite possible to wire up the relays without using pcbs but for neatness, simplicity and straightforward wiring there is much to commend them. Faultfinding, too becomes easier when the mass of interconnecting wires is eliminated.

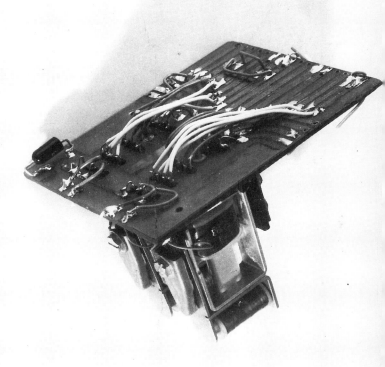

38 (*Above*) A latching relay. The two coils can be seen that operate the two sides of the switching mechanism. The curved bank of contacts are located in the lower compartment of the device.

39 (*Right*) Two latching relays mounted on a home-made printed circuit board.

(5mm) and this is the basis of the dimensions shown for the switch slide and contact panel. On the prototype the spring wire contacts were thin brass wire turned over on top of the contact panel and fixed with epoxy glue to prevent them from rotating.

You may experience some difficulty in obtaining latching relays. They appear to be ex-GPO or military stock, and you can sometimes find them in surplus stores dealing with this type of equipment. Many of the electronic component stores will be able to put you in touch with a source, and may also help with the alternative double-throw relay. For those who would like to make their own, it is possible to do so using an ordinary turnout motor (see figure 40). The throw of the driving pin on the Peco model is just $\frac{3}{16}$in

Printed circuit board

A method of making your own pcb is described below. You can either use a kit which contains all the necessary materials, or buy the materials individually. Sources from which they may be obtained are given on page 134.

Let us assume that a bank of five relays are provided for a five block system. You will need a piece of single-faced copper laminate board about 8in × 4in (200mm × 100mm). Polish the copper face of the board with fine

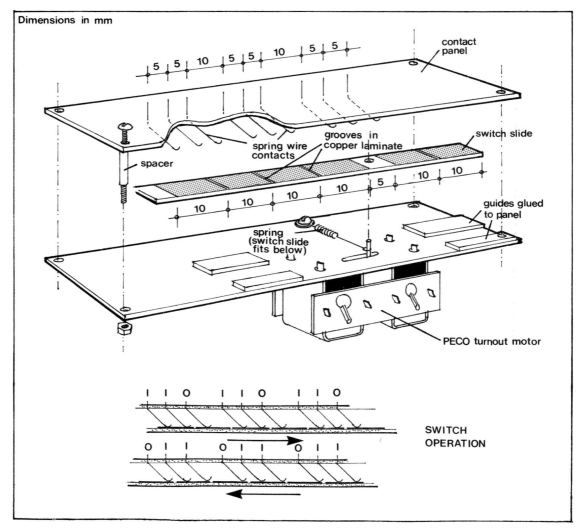

Dimensions in mm

contact panel

spring wire contacts

grooves in copper laminate

switch slide

spacer

guides glued to panel

spring (switch slide fits below)

PECO turnout motor

SWITCH OPERATION

40 An alternative to the latching relay, using a turnout motor.

wire wool until it is really shiny, then wipe it over with methylated spirits to remove any traces of grease. Cover the entire copper face with strips of masking tape, and then carefully ink in the circuit board layout on to the masking tape. Mark the location of all holes, and drill these to the appropriate size before beginning the next step. Using a modelling knife and a straight edge, cut around the marked panels and remove the masking tape covering the areas of copper *that are to remain.* You will now have exposed the copper pattern of the circuit board, while the portions to be etched away are still covered by the masking tape. Now paint over the entire surface – copper as well as masking tape – with cellulose paint. Car touch-up paint is satisfactory – the brush-on variety is better than the spray. When the paint is completely dry and hardened, perhaps a day later, peel off the (painted) masking tape, being careful not to touch the newly-exposed copper surface.

The copper panels which are to remain are now protected with cellulose paint. Check that there are no unwanted bridges between panels, and do any necessary touching up. Then immerse the whole panel in a dish of etching fluid, which is a strong solution of ferric chloride in water to which has been added a small amount of hydrochloric acid – the quantities are not critical. This is a toxic solution which must be stored away safely from unauthorised hands, in a plastic or glass bottle with a plastic stopper. Use rubber gloves while handling the circuit board at this stage.

A substitution reaction takes place – the ferric chloride + copper becomes copper chloride + iron. The copper chloride goes into solution while the iron is precipitated; it is necessary to agitate the board from time to time to prevent this precipitate from impeding the reaction. After about half an hour the exposed copper will be etched away and the colour of the board below will show through. Check that this stage has been reached by removing the board and washing it in cold running water.

Now remove the cellulose paint by rubbing over with wire wool again, and then wash and examine the whole board. Ensure that there are no unwanted copper connections between panels.

Wiring and assembling the circuit board (figure 41)

The latching relays may now be mounted on the reverse side of the pcb, using epoxy resin glue. Ensure that the fixing prongs and all the terminals are correctly located in the holes previously drilled. Now wire the resistors for the signal lamp circuits to the board and fit the 220Ω resistors on the reverse side, with their wires pulled through the holes and soldered to the copper panels.

Connect up the terminals of the latching relays by soldering short lengths of insulated wire between them and the appropriate panels. Follow the diagram carefully, checking the work as you proceed and again at completion.

The whole unit is now ready to be wired into your layout. As access to it will rarely be necessary, it may be fitted in some convenient out-of-the-way location, provided that this does not make the initial wiring too awkward. In order to protect the contacts from dust enclose the latching relays in a sealed box such as a plastic freezer container. This can be taped in position or held with long screws or bolts.

Connecting the control unit to the trackwork

Begin the installation by connecting up the circuit that operates the relays. You will need a mains transformer with a tapping giving about 33v to energize the electromagnets. As all relay ratings will not necessarily match those of the prototype, you will need to experiment to determine the optimum voltage. As only momentary pulses of power will be used, the voltage is not critical, and you will find that the coils function satisfactorily over a fairly wide range. If your transformer has a number of tappings, start by connecting up the lowest voltage and, using a test prod, increase the power until the electromagnets operate smartly and positively. Once you have determined the best pair of terminals, solder an insulated wire to one of them and connect this to one side of each of the reed switches in turn.

The reed switches must be located immediately after the track isolator in each

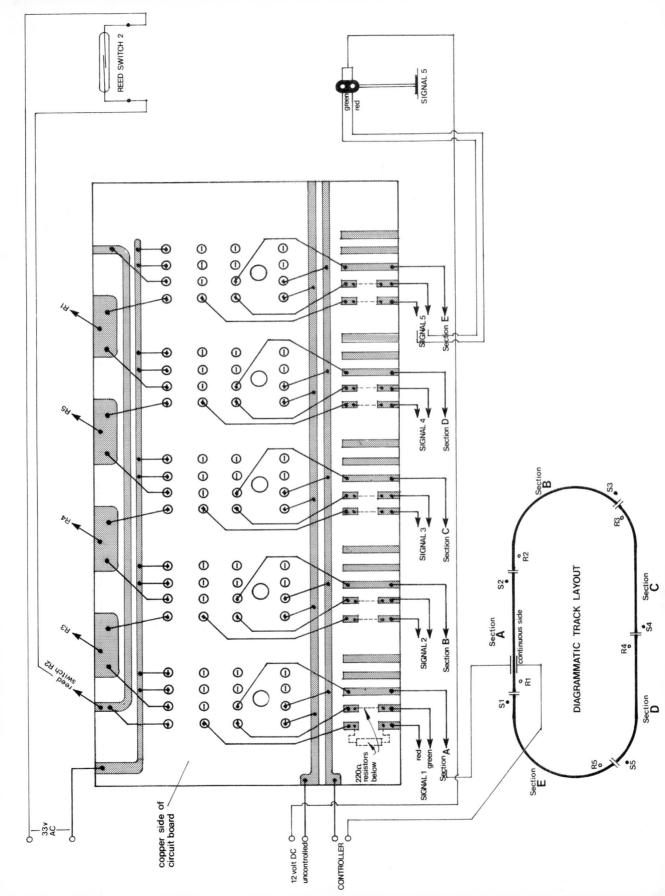

REED SWITCH 2

green
red

SIGNAL 5

R1

R5

R4

R3

reed switch R2

33v AC

copper side of circuit board

SIGNAL 5
Section E

SIGNAL 4
Section D

SIGNAL 3
Section C

SIGNAL 2
Section B

220Ω resistors below

red
green

SIGNAL 1
Section A

12 volt DC
uncontrolled

CONTROLLER

Section A
continuous side

S1
R1

S2
R2

Section B

S3
R3

Section C

S4
R4

R5
S5

Section D

Section E

DIAGRAMMATIC TRACK LAYOUT

41 Wiring and assembly of circuit board for a block control system.

section, and set in position so that the reeds close when a magnet is passed over the top of them. As the ends where the wires pass through the glass envelope of the switches are potentially weak points, some care is needed in preparing them. Hold each wire firmly in a pair of needle-nosed pliers close up to the glass and bend the free end down at right angles, ensuring that each pair of wires points in the same direction and that the reeds lie one over the other. Measure off the distance between the wires, drill two holes in the baseboard between the sleepers and push the reed switch into position. A dab of epoxy resin glue will secure the switch firmly (see figure 42). The whole assembly can later be painted over to match the track treatment without affecting its operation.

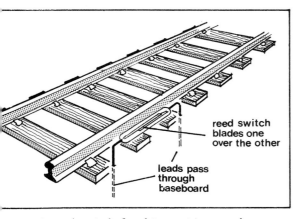

reed switch blades one over the other

leads pass through baseboard

42 A reed switch fitted in position on the trackwork for block control.

Now connect the remaining wire of each of the reed switches to the appropriate terminal on the block control board. Switch on the mains supply to the transformer and test the unit by passing a magnet over each of the reed switches in turn.

It is easy to fix a small cylindrical magnet to a convenient point on the underside of the train with epoxy resin glue, but its location needs some carefully consideration. It looks less unsightly if the magnet is fixed on the far side, away from the usual direction of observation, but you may not wish to attach it to the locomotive at all. One of the carriages or wagons will serve equally as well, or you could fix it between the wheels of the locomotive. Whatever you choose to do, ensure that the combination of the reed switch and the magnet causes the train to stop in precisely the position you have determined.

The positive terminal of the 12v uncontrolled supply outlet of the controller is taken to the block control board, and the leads to the red and green lamps of the signals are connected up. Finally the negative terminal is taken to each of the signal common return leads. It is essential to use colour-coded wires for the connections between the pcb and track to avoid confusion.

In order to introduce a degree of manual control to this automatic system, it is useful to have a set of push-to-make buttons on the main control panel, which are connected in parallel with each of the reed switches. This will enable you to stop and start trains at the end of each section if required. This action will not interfere with the 'safety' aspect of the automatics, and a train stopped manually will still be protected by a 'dead' section of track immediately behind it.

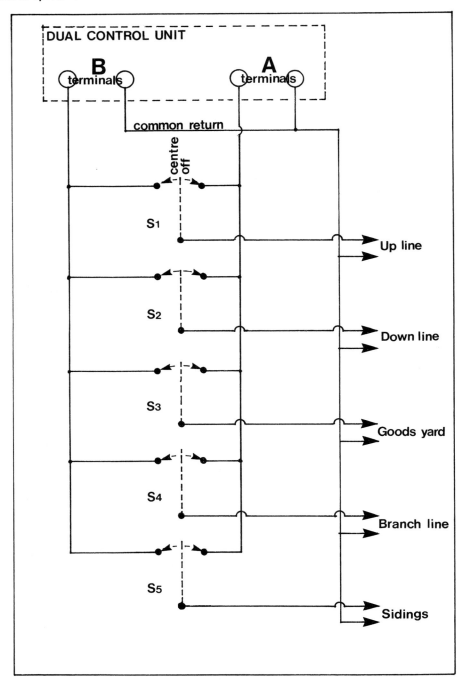

43 Switching arrangement for control of track
sections by either of the dual controls on the
master controller.

Terminal connections

At the track end of the wiring system you will find the most positive and successful means of making a connection with the rails is simply to solder the wires to the *outside* of the track and take them below the baseboard through small holes drilled between the sleepers. Rust-coloured paint (see page 41) will adequately disguise the blobs of solder.

At the control panel end you will find it convenient to have a switching arrangement which allows each section of track to be connected to either the A or B outlets of the main controller unit. This can be used in a number of ways. You might have two trains running on control A, and wish to bring a third out of the station slowly across a network of turnouts. Control B can be used for this, and once the third train has attained cruising speed it can be switched over to join the two already on control A. This will leave control B free to operate other trains. You will need a two-way switch for each circuit, preferably with a *centre-off* position. A circuit diagram is shown in figure 43.

44 A circuit providing gradual slowing down before stopping. Be sure that you connect the diodes D1 and D2 the right way round.

Realistic slowing down

If the controller is set to a satisfactory operating speed and a train enters a dead section of track, the instant stopping is less than realistic. In reality, passengers would fly across the compartments into their fellow travellers, and in the restaurant cars soup-stained diners would be crawling from beneath the tables! It is possible to introduce a refinement to overcome this situation (see figure 44).

An additional isolator is inserted into the track some 300mm (12in) from the main section isolator. A 220 Ω resistor R1 is fitted across this isolator in series with a diode D1 (BY126), and a similar diode D2 across the main isolator, but facing the other way. If section B is switched off, a train entering subsection A will drawn current through R1 causing it to slow down and eventually stop when it reaches section B. However, if section B is switched on, subsection A is charged through D2 to the full voltage, and a train will proceed from section A to section B without slowing down. D1 prevents section A when switched off from becoming charged through D2.

This simple arrangement installed at each point of isolation will give realistic slowing down without adjusting the setting of the main controller. The components may be concealed discreetly beneath the baseboard. Take care that the diodes are installed the right way around.

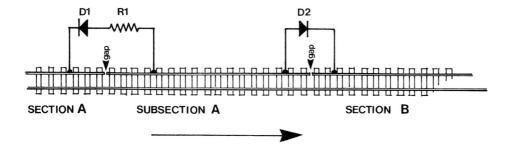

SECTION **A**   SUBSECTION **A**   SECTION **B**

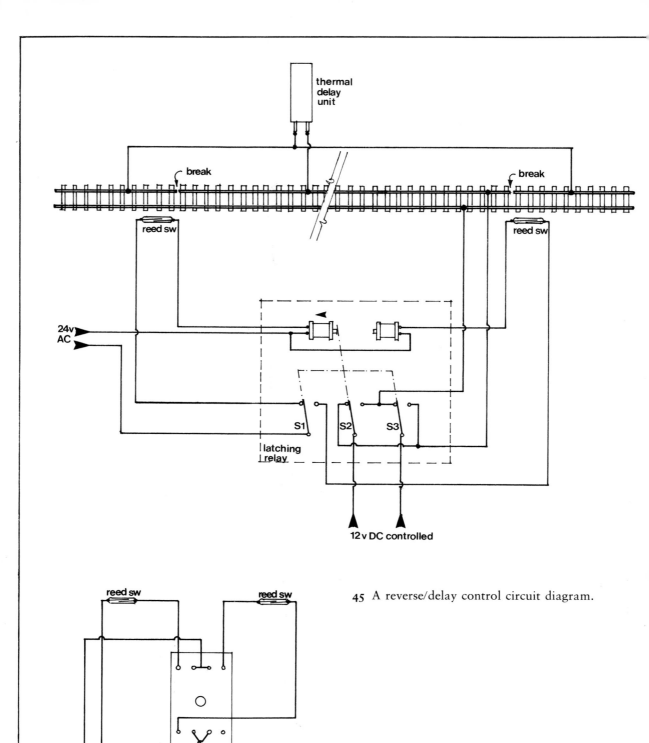

45 A reverse/delay control circuit diagram.

Automatic delay and reverse control unit

Where an end-to-end line is incorporated in a layout, such as a branch line, it can be useful to instal automatic control. This will allow a train to travel to the terminus station, pause for a period, and then return to the other end of the line, where it will again pause and reverse.

You will need a latching relay (figure 38), two reed switches and a thermal delay unit. There are two or three of the latter available, including one marketed by Fleischmann.

The theoretical circuit is shown in figure 45. A short section of track is required at the two ends of the line, each having one isolated rail; to these is connected one terminal of the delay unit. The other terminal is connected to the rail between the isolated sections. Because the polarity of the line will need to be reversed, it is important to remember to isolate totally this part of the layout from any other part using the common return system.

The reed switches must be positioned so that the magnet attached to the train will operate them at the same time as, or fractionally after, the isolated section is entered. As the reed switch is operated, the circuit causes both the polarity of the track to be reversed and the reverse switching facility to be transferred to the reed switch at the other end of the line.

Once the wiring has been completed, place a locomotive on the centre section of the track and turn the controller to give forward movement. The locomotive will move towards the end of the track and stop as it enters the isolated section, as the thermal delay begins to function. If everything has been correctly connected up the locomotive will move off in reverse at the end of the delay period and travel to the other end of the track, where the same routine will be followed. If not, reverse the terminals connected to the track and try again – or simply switch the controller to reverse.

Turnout operation

There are a number of manufacturers who market turnouts with varying degrees of realism. For compatibility it is obviously advantageous to use turnouts of the same manufacture as the trackwork. Peco *Streamline Insulfrog Universal* turnouts are integrated units with the sleeper base moulded on to the rails. The turnout blades are pivoted for smooth, free movement and the tie-rod is fitted with over-centre springing for positive action. They are self-isolating, which means that current is automatically directed the way that the turnout faces (see figure 46). This is particularly useful for sidings where it may be desirable to isolate the track on which a spare locomotive stands.

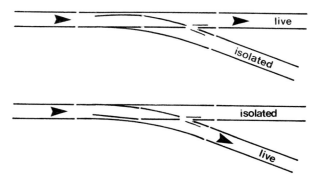

46 Operation of self-isolating turnout. The current is automatically directed the way that the turnout faces.

Once fitted the turnouts are ready for manual operation; but for busy areas of the layout it is recommended that turnout motors are used, which permit operation from the main control panel. These are located out of sight below the baseboard *at the time the trackwork is laid*. Full instructions for mounting and wiring are given with each motor.

Wiring these motors is a fairly straightforward procedure. Connect together one terminal on each of the two solenoids and take this to the 16vAC outlet of the controller. The other terminals are each connected *via* a colour coded wire to the two sides of a *passing contact* switch (such as the Peco Lectrics switch). The centre terminal of the passing contact switch completes the circuit by being connected to the 16v AC outlet (see figure 47).

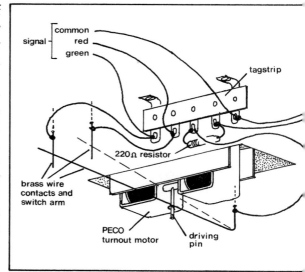

48 A switch for a signal light operated by a turnout motor.

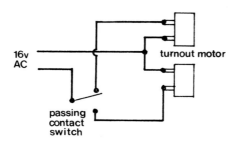

47 Wiring a turnout motor.

You can protect the motors against burnout by inserting a capacitor discharge unit into the circuit – only one is required for the whole layout. This inexpensive device is well worth including, and it has the additional advantage of giving very positive motor action.

Automatic signal operation

To add realism, display a red signal to stop approaching trains at sections of track that have been isolated by operating a turnout. A simple switch operated by the turnout itself can be constructed as shown in figure 48. An example of the use of this switch is seen in

figure 49, designed to avoid a collision at the crossover. A train on the down line has been directed to the sidings. A switch, operated by the motor of turnout T1, has isolated the section shown as a broken line. A second switch on the same motor has changed the signal S2 to red. As a result, a train on the up line will wait at the red signal until the turnout T1 is restored to facing the down line again.

Signal lights

There are a variety of signal types available from model railway shops, some with excellent and realistic detail. For those who wish to make their own, details are given in figure 50. It is easy to obtain 12v grain-of-wheat bulbs, which are suitable for these signals. The life of these tiny lamps can be considerably extended by under-loading them, reducing the current by inserting a 220Ω resistor in the circuit.

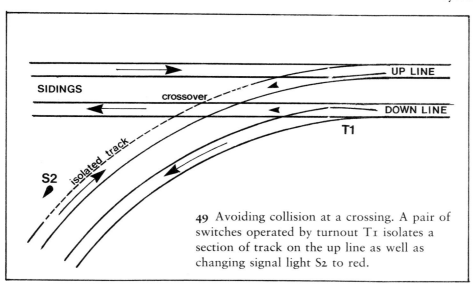

49 Avoiding collision at a crossing. A pair of switches operated by turnout T1 isolates a section of track on the up line as well as changing signal light S2 to red.

50 A two-lamp signal light.

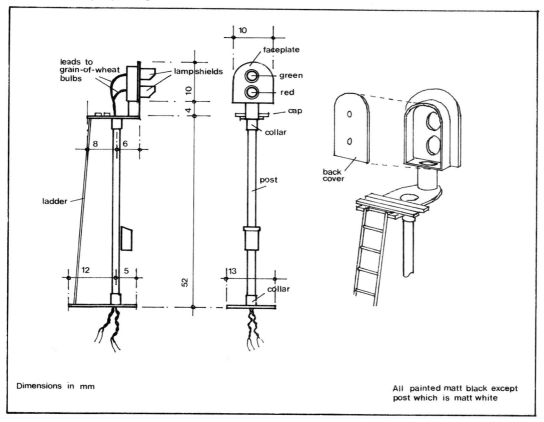

Dimensions in mm

All painted matt black except post which is matt white

The base, faceplate and cap of the signal are made of Plasticard, while the post, postbase, collar and lamp shields are aluminium tube. Ladders are either ready-made etched brass or Ratio plastic. Push the two pairs of wires from the bulbs down the post, and fit the bulbs into their respective shields, remembering that green goes at the top. Paint the whole assembly matt black except for the post between the postbase and collar, which is matt white.

The design can be modified to make double-headed or multiple-lamp signals, gantry suspended or bracket types or any of the many designs encountered in a railway control system.

51 *Ratio* LNER lattice post OO gauge signals have been modelled with faithful attention to the detail of the prototype. All four of these signals are available in one kit. (*Courtesy of Ratio Plastic Models Limited*)

Install the signals facing the left-hand side of an approaching train, allowing sufficient clearance for the widest locomotive or other item of rolling stock. Drill a hole through the baseboard and feed the signal wires down through it. Apply a small quantity of pva glue to the underside of the baseplate, and rest the jaws of a pair of pliers on it while the glue sets. Ensure that the post is vertical. Screw a small tagstrip to the underside of the baseboard and solder to it the signal wires and the connecting leads from the control panel.

Semaphore signals

If the period of your layout and your dedication to accuracy prohibit the use of signal lights, use semaphore signals instead. These are available in every imaginable form – including kits; ready-made, non-operating,

52 This OO gauge SR home and distant signal by *Ratio* comes in a partly assembled pre-coloured kit. (*Courtesy of Ratio Plastic Models Limited*)

tube and wire ones; as well as electrically operated types – in each of the various company outlines. (A realistic scale kit at a very modest price is marketed by Ratio Plastic Models Ltd., and this can be adapted for push-wire or electrical control.) There have been a number of ingenious articles on adaptation in the *Railway Modeller* magazine over the years, one of the most recent being in the April 1986 edition. The principle of these adaptations is the use of a turnout motor below the baseboard which moves a T-shaped crank, giving the necessary direction of movement to the signal arm. However, many modellers are content to instal non-working signals of the correct type to their layouts, simply as part of the scenic background.

53 Street lighting using fibre optics.

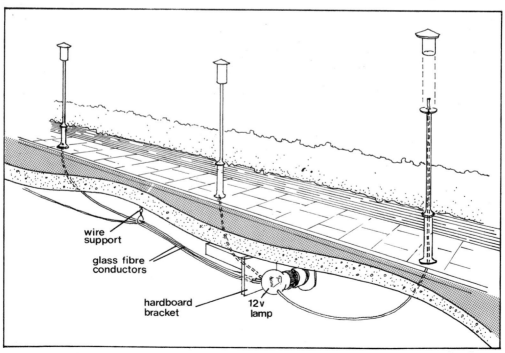

wire
support

glass fibre
conductors

hardboard
bracket

12v
lamp

Street lighting

Bulbs fitted above entrance alcoves to buildings and other out-of-the-way places can provide an acceptable level of street lighting to the layout. If you intend installing functioning lamp-posts, consistency demands a considerable number, with a consequent effect on your budget. It is cheaper to use *glass fibre conductors*, known as *fibre optics*, which are available in a range of gauges and lengths. Several fibres are used to conduct the light from one bulb concealed beneath the baseboard to a number of lamp-posts or other lighting fittings. The effect of a large number of tiny points of light, while not actually giving any illumination, can be quite dramatic.

Building lighting

Using adhesive tape or otherwise fixing a grain-of-wheat bulb and its resistor inside some or all of the buildings greatly enhances the appearance of the layout, particularly if the general lighting in the model room can be switched off or dimmed. Group the wires to the bulbs together in a random fashion in order to reduce the number of switches on the control panel, and vary the resistors between $100\,\Omega$ and $300\,\Omega$ to give a range of lighting levels. Bulbs may be concealed beneath the station canopies to give illumination to the platforms.

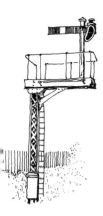

4 Landscaping

The introduction of scenery and landscaping to railway modelling was the principal factor in differentiating between the train set temporarily laid out on the floor and the scale model railway layout on its own baseboard with the railway forming an integral part of a realistic scenic setting. The demand for realism and accuracy of detail has done much to induce manufacturers to take great care over the design and construction of their products. The resultant availability of a wide range of modelling materials has done much to aid the modeller in his quest for realism.

While the construction of locomotives, rolling stock and buildings calls for skill and accuracy to obtain acceptable results, the whole undertaking of landscaping is a good deal less precise. Artistic skill, while helpful, is by no means essential. The artist working on canvas may have to create a scene which gives an illusion of depth while working in only two dimensions, whereas on a three-dimensional layout this faculty is not essential. If clumsy work with a knife reduces a section of bank at the trackside rather more than intended, a dab of plaster will put it right; or you may decide that the irregularity is not out of keeping with what might be expected in reality. Perhaps the most useful skill in building a realistic scene is that of observation, and in conjunction with this there is the useful *aide-memoire* of the colour photograph.

You will find it most helpful to study photographs and read articles on the subject of building model landscapes. The magazine *Railway Modeller* carries a wealth of such information each month. Exhibition layouts are also a source of useful instruction, and careful observation will often give you ideas that can be adapted to suit your own model. Many museums – for example, the Science Museum in London – have *dioramas* which, while not necessarily depicting railways, are worth your researching in order to see how professional model landscapers depict a scene. Displays of architectural models, too, generally incorporate a degree of landscaping, and are worth studying. In all of these you should note what provisions are made for lighting, for a good model is wasted if displayed in poor light.

Tools

The tools required for landscaping are fairly unsophisticated, and are of the type readily available to the do-it-yourself enthusiast. You will need:

- A saw for cutting up larger sheets of material, a hand or electric drill and a set of bits, a few screwdrivers and possibly a hammer.
- An electric jigsaw which is very useful for cutting curved contour lines, but is by no means essential.

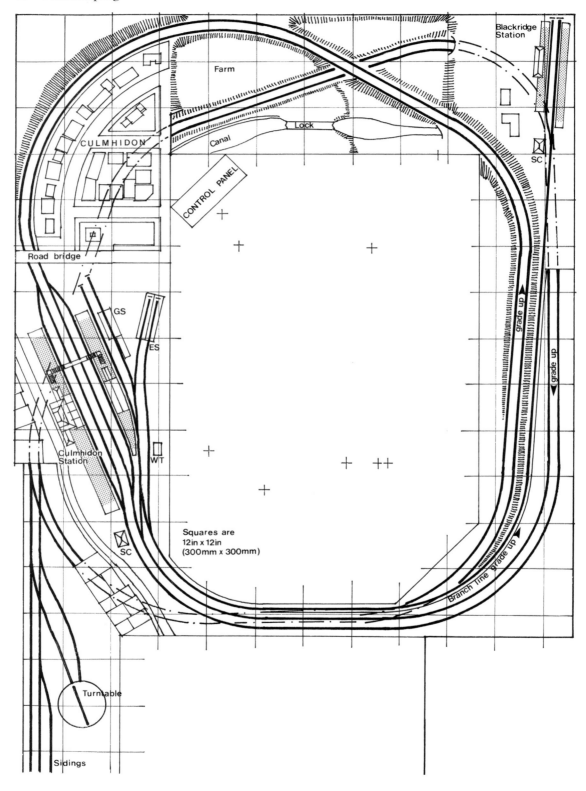

Blackridge
Station

Farm

Lock

Canal

CULMHIDON

CONTROL PANEL

Road bridge

GS

ES

Culmhidon
Station

WT

SC

Squares are
12in x 12in
(300mm x 300mm)

grade up

grade up

Branch line grade up

SC

Turntable

Sidings

54 The author's loft layout plan. This is called a looped figure eight configuration, each track on the main lines making two circuits before returning to the starting point. The branch line to Blackridge station at the highest level is single track, and can be interconnnected with the down line *via* the turnouts at Culmhidon station.

- For smaller scale work a large craft knife with spare blades as well as a modelling knife with a selection of different blades.
- A few paint brushes, ranging from about 1in (25mm) down to a fairly fine one for detailed work. Some of these brushes will be used for applying glue, so good quality ones are unnecessary.

Planning

It must be stressed again that you should not make a start on landscaping your layout until you have a reasonably firm overall plan for the final result. Clearly, minor modifications are inevitable as the work proceeds, but avoid the introduction of major changes once the work is well under way. Much of the landscape work is fragile, and attempting to cut out sections to allow alterations to the layout can cause a great deal of damage.

Any modeller sets out to create an impression of reality. In the case of a railway layout, however good the scenic work, much of the effect will be lost if the train is seen to be circulating on a continuous track. The aim should be to give the appearance that the trains are actually going somewhere. This can be achieved by the use of deep cuttings and tunnels, so that a train disappears for a period, to emerge later in an unexpected place. A multi-level layout using a looped figure-of-eight configuration and several independently-operated trains helps to give this effect (see figure 54).

Backscene panel

The object of a backscene panel is to avoid the appearance of the layout coming to an abrupt end at the back edge of the baseboard. The construction of a support for this panel is described on page 34. If you have a flair for painting and a basic understanding of perspective, you may wish to try your talents in this area, whether it be townscape or rolling country scenery. For parts of the backscene that represent the space closest to the modelled landscape, a good effect can be obtained by using the same scatter materials on both the model and the backscene (see figure 55). The colours must become more muted as the scene recedes to enhance the illusion of perspective.

An alternative method is to use printed sheets of scenic backgrounds. These are designed to allow any sheet to be joined to another to form a continuous background scene.

Whichever method you choose, you should consider the final relation between backscene and model at this stage, so that the one becomes an extension of the other. You will then be able to blend your colours in such a way that the two elements merge properly.

Basic contours

Very little of a natural landscape is completely flat. Even where such a condition is desired, there will be minor bumps in the ground level, and these should be modelled in the interests of reality.

It is usually unnecessary to go to the expense of purchasing materials for the construction of basic contours. You will probably have scrap materials left over from the construction of baseboards, or perhaps pieces of ceiling board, which can be used for

55 The same scatter material has been used on the landscaping and the backdrop to help them merge and give an appearance of depth.

56 (*Below*) With the baseboards and trackwork complete, the plan of the canal and lock is used to set out the first area for landscaping. Note the OO gauge measuring scale, used a great deal at this stage.

contour formers. One method of building is to cut the contours from this material, which is generally ½in (12mm) thick, and screw them down one on top of another to the baseboard (see figure 57). The edges of the boards can be splayed off by a large sharp craft knife where necessary, or treated as described on page 74. Expanded polystyrene in the form of ceiling tiles or packaging slabs is another suitable and easily carved product for use in this context. It is essential to use the recommended adhesive when fixing this material.

57 (*Below top*) Fibreboard contours form the gentle fall of the farm, while steeper parts are built up with vertical card formers.

58 (*Below bottom*) The vertical formers are covered with layers of newspaper.

Another method is to use vertical formers cut from either ½in (12mm) fibreboard, hardboard or corrugated cardboard. (An abundance of corrugated cardboard containers is usually available at your local supermarket.) Cut out the formers and glue them with pva glue to the baseboard no more than 3in (75mm) apart. Small pieces of card should then be glued between the formers to give an egg carton effect, so that the span of the covering material is kept to a minimum.

Where access to the particular contoured area is restricted, you will find it a good deal easier to work 'off-site'. Cut a piece of hardboard to the shape of the base layout of the area and glue the formers to it as shown in figure 59. In this case, complete the scene down to the last detail before lifting it into position on the layout.

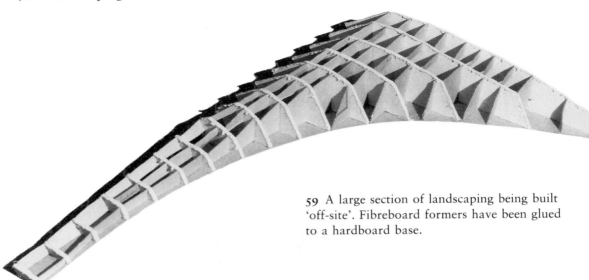

59 A large section of landscaping being built 'off-site'. Fibreboard formers have been glued to a hardboard base.

60 The formers are covered with layers of newspaper dipped in wallpaper paste.

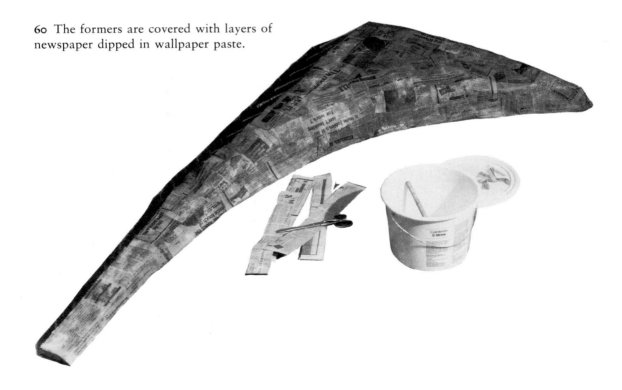

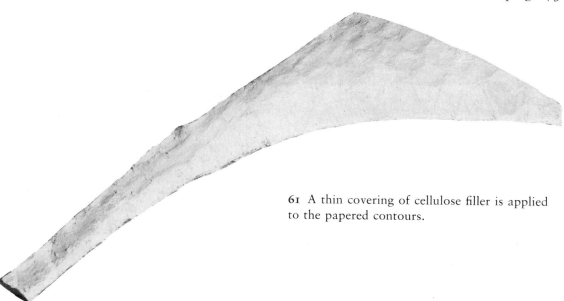

61 A thin covering of cellulose filler is applied to the papered contours.

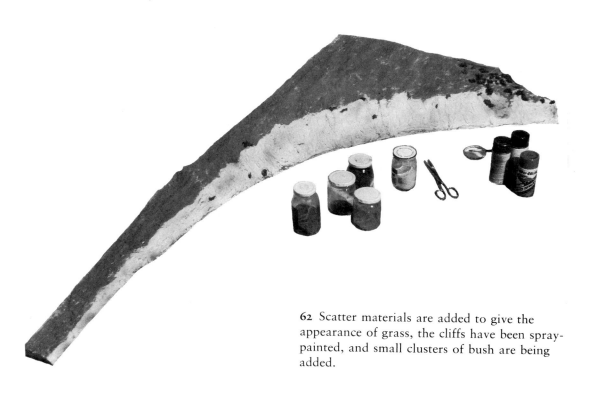

62 Scatter materials are added to give the appearance of grass, the cliffs have been spray-painted, and small clusters of bush are being added.

Contour covering

Once the glue holding the formers has set, the covering material may be applied. Mix a stiff paste of wallpaper glue and apply this with your fingers to strips of paper (the *Radio Times* is ideal) about 2in (50mm) wide. Lay the strips in a criss-cross fashion across the formers, building the covering up to about three thicknesses to give strength. Pull the strips tight as you proceed to avoid sagging between the formers (see figure 60).

The whole construction must now be left until quite dry, probably for several days. It will then be strong enough to be lifted without buckling, and will feel firm and sound hollow when tapped.

Now smear a thin paste of cellulose filler over the paper covering. (You may feel this unnecessary, in which case proceed with colouring and finishing the surface.) Cellulose filler serves a useful purpose in covering the print on the paper and in simulating outcrops of rock or earth in amongst the grass (see figure 61).

The papering and plastering method described above is useful to slope off the vertical edges of horizontal layers of fibreboard where this method of contouring has been used.

Another method of building up the landscape is to use a fine mesh wire netting, such as aviary wire, stapled to the fibreboard formers. This can be pressed into the required shape, and is particularly useful where building a rugged terrain. Then cover the netting with strips of plaster bandage that have been briefly dipped in water. Mould the bandage into shape with your fingers as you go along, although remember its quick-drying property! *Mod-Roc* is a good example of this material. Alternatively, strips of newspaper or kitchen roll may be dipped into a creamy mixture of cellulose filler and laid across the netting to give a similar result.

Surface detailing

If you apply scatter materials directly to the contour covering, you will need a generous quantity to prevent the newsprint or white plaster showing through. It is more satisfactory to paint first the covering green with poster or emulsion paint. Even watercolour may be used to give brown-yellow colours which show through the grass finish. A very light spray with aerosol paint can be effective; use the matt brown spray available for undercoating car body repairs. Grey and black are also available in this range and have a variety of uses. The remainder of car aerosols have a gloss finish and are not really suitable unless used very sparingly, as the gloss prevents even glueing of the scatter materials.

It is helpful to refer to photographs of scenic models, and indeed to the real thing, to help you in your endeavours to obtain credible results in your modelling. Colour is extremely important, particularly the way in which it constantly varies. Seldom, if ever, is a field of grass or a rock face one uniform shade.

Rock

A good method of achieving a rocky wall face is first to apply a generous layer of cellulose filler mix over the base construction and then to press into it a crumpled sheet of aluminium kitchen foil. Work in fairly small areas at a time, or the plaster will dry before you have textured it. After a few minutes remove the foil to reveal the desired faceted appearance. The same foil can be used repeatedly. You may find it necessary to do some touching up with plaster to get exactly the right result. Real pieces of stone can be glued to the model or embedded in plaster, the sharply-angled

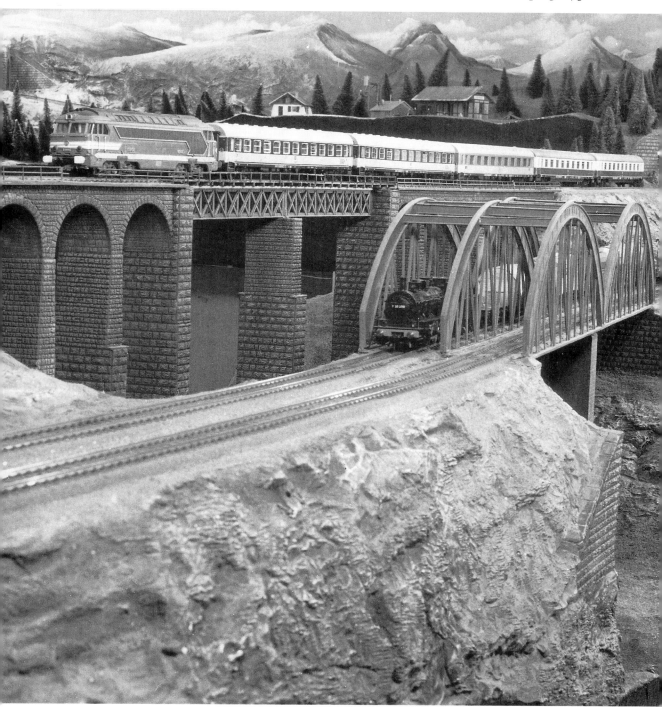

63 Some excellent rock effects on one of the displays at the Pecorama exhibition. Note the stonework on the viaduct and the realistic scenic backdrop. (*Courtesy of Peco Studios*)

variety such as slate or flint being better than rounded ones. Cork bark is a popular material for simulating a striated rock effect, and is readily obtainable at most model shops. There is great scope for experimenting at this stage with other materials that you feel might have possibilities.

Now mix some black poster colour with white emulsion paint to obtain a medium grey colour. Paint this over the plasterwork and allow it to dry. Take a matt black aerosol spray and spray a very small amount on to the work from one side, at a steep angle. The protruding pieces of rock will be darkened, while the areas shaded by the protrusions remain grey. Use great discretion in the application of the spray, and stand back at frequent intervals to examine the result critically. When satisfied, add some small patches of various shades of brown in some of the crevices and on upper surfaces. A few fine vertical white streaks might indicate the presence of nesting sea-birds. You can obtain the effect of lichen by dipping a stick into yellow ochre paint and drawing it across the bristles of an old toothbrush, causing the paint to spatter on to the rock. Finally paint a few lines of pva glue on crevices and ledges and sprinkle on green flock powder to give the effect of plant life.

Chalk cliffs can be effectively represented by your painting a very thin wash of grey over the plasterwork, and then applying minute quantities of black and brown aerosol sprays as already described. Apply small amounts of greenery as before.

Grass

The basic method of grassing the model is as follows: mix roughly equal quantities of pva glue and water. Paint this on to an area of the model no more than 6in (150mm) square, and immediately sprinkle over the wet glue either flock powder or scenic dressing material until all the moisture has been soaked up. Leave unglued those areas where earth or rock is to show through the grass. Continue painting and sprinkling until the whole area has been completed. The scenic dressing is considerably coarser than the flock, and gives a much rougher texture suitable for pastures and farmland. Use at least three colours of dressing or flock randomly to give the proper degree of variation. If too much has been added, vacuum away the excess once the glue has dried, holding the nozzle of the cleaner a few inches above the surface. If you want to retrieve this material for use elsewhere, the toe of a pair of tights pushed into the nozzle of the vacuum cleaner tube makes a handy collection bag. (Do obtain the consent of the owner of the tights before carrying out this procedure!) Some brightly coloured flocks are available – yellows and mauves – which you can apply very sparingly over the grass to represent wildflowers. If the final result needs toning down, a quick spray with a matt black aerosol spray is effective.

You may care to try your hand at making your own scatter materials. Fine sawdust, or even the powder obtained from a sanding wheel, can be dyed to the desired colour with cold-water dyes; you must then spread the material out on newspaper afterwards to dry. The particles tend to stick together, but you can separate them when completely dry by placing a cupful at a time in a liquidiser for a few moments.

Having now completed the grass, it is necessary to add the finishing touches. You can reproduce small bushes and other low growth by fixing down small quantities of model foliage material with spots of pva glue. Represent isolated rocks by pieces of gravel.

Trees

Trees can add a great deal of realism to your model, and undoubtedly you will need a fair number of them before the model looks complete. And even at that stage you may find that a rather bare area would benefit by the addition of a few extra trees.

The first consideration is whether to buy ready-made model trees or to build your own. A number of manufacturers provide a wide range of products from complete trees ready to be planted straight on to the layout, to kits that enable you to make a variety of tree types. The range varies from authentic looking models down to the so-called bottle-brush trees, which look exactly like bottle-brushes.

The best of these models are marketed by John Piper (Accessories) Ltd., who cover both ready-made and kit form trees. They also manufacture sheets of etched brass leaves of actual species – to scale! – which are perhaps the ultimate in realism. Woodland Scenics also produce a realistic range of indigenous tree models as well as model foliage material.

However, while the cost of a few of these models is not excessive, you may well have to consider the expense involved in installing a large number of them. There is also the matter of the overall impression given by the layout: an isolated tree in the foreground will obviously attract attention and will need to be to a high standard of modelling, while a group forming a small wood at the back of the model probably need be only rudimentary. If you decide to make your own trees you can apportion the amount of time and care required to suit each particular location. Alternatively, you can spend more money on good foreground models and use cheaper types in less exposed situations.

Simple trees can be made quite quickly from suitable twigs, which represent the trunk and main branches. Glue on pieces of dyed lichen or model foliage with pva glue. This produces an adequate tree for the background of the model where several could form a small wood. Another even simpler method of making bushes or small trees is to collect the fluffy white seed of the *wild clematis* (old man's beard) from hedgerows during the winter months. Aerosol spraying

64 Outlines of a few indigenous British trees.

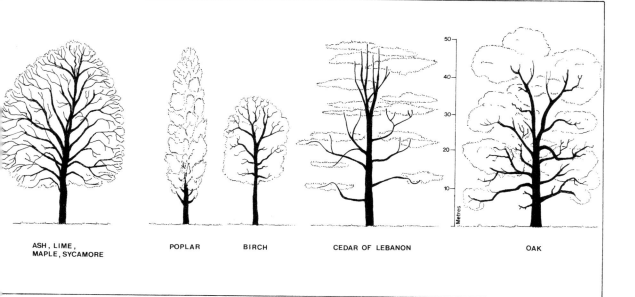

ASH, LIME,
MAPLE, SYCAMORE   POPLAR   BIRCH   CEDAR OF LEBANON   OAK

these green produces a reasonably effective result, suitable once again for background or groups. Hedgerows are a source of a number of useful materials for your landscape, and a careful look at twigs and plant stems will surely give you some ideas.

Making a really good, convincing tree is not as difficult as you might imagine. It needs a little patience and time, but if you adopt a mass production method, making, say, a dozen at a time, you will achieve a surprisingly quick result. By using the procedure described you have the opportunity to make not only distinct tree species, but also examples of specific trees, should you so desire. As in all scenery construction, it is better to base the work on photographs you have taken or on illustrations you have culled from various publications.

A few outlines of trees common to the British landscape are given in figure 64. It is interesting to note that while many of these grow to a considerable size, trees on models which exceed 35 to 40ft (10 to 12m) in height look disproportionately large. You should therefore confine yourself to this maximum even if you base your model on a particular, taller tree.

You will need fairly fine wire for the trunk and branches. The shellac-insulated 30 gauge wire used for transformer and receiver coil windings is about right. (The whole procedure is illustrated in figures 65 to 74.) Cut a piece of corrugated cardboard two or three inches wide to the tree height required. A length of 6in (150mm) will give a 35ft (10m) high tree. Wind the wire lengthwise around the cardboard about 40 full turns. Bend the cardboard to assist the removal of the wire and cut through all the strands at one end. Twist the other ends of the wire tightly together for about a quarter of the way up the tree and then draw off perhaps a dozen strands to form the first branch. Twist these strands together, always turning in the same

direction to avoid unravelling earlier twisting. After a little more twisting, separate out a few more strands. Continue twisting and separating until single strands are left. Work your way up the tree in this manner until you have constructed the whole trunk and branch system. Now brush a little PVA glue over part of the trunk and immediately sprinkle flock powder over the wet glue to give body and texture. The colour of the flock is not particularly important as it is later to be painted, but if a green or grey is used small areas can be left showing through the paintwork to represent lichen or moss. Continue the glue and flock process until the trunk and main branches have been covered. Put the model aside until the glue has set – preferably overnight – and then paint it with matt enamel to the colour required. Tree trunks vary in colour greatly, from grey to brown to green, and you must choose the colour that will relate best to the surroundings you are creating. Quite often the north sides of tree trunks in exposed places are a bright green because of moss growth.

Many trees have a dark green covering of ivy on their trunks, which you can simulate by painting: stippling on the leaves, and using fine brushstrokes to represent the ivy stems. Your own observations will provide you with many peculiarities which you can incorporate in the interests of authenticity.

Foliage is required to finish the model. Three methods are here described, the first being the most realistic.

● Model foliage (such as Woodland Scenics foliage) appears to be a mixture of finely divided coloured rubbery particles and incredibly thin filaments of nylon. It is available either light or dark green, and gives a very realistic appearance. Cut small thumbnail-sized irregular pieces of the material and then tease them out to a lacy consistency. Secure them to the branches by means of spots of PVA glue. Keep turning

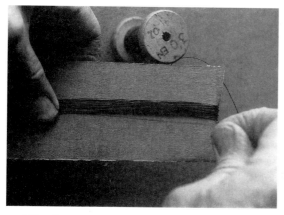

65 The first stage in making a tree. Wire is being wound on a card to give the required height of the tree.

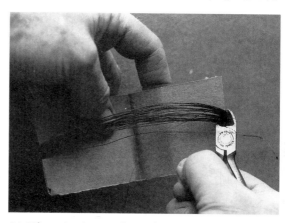

66 The wire is cut through at one end of the card.

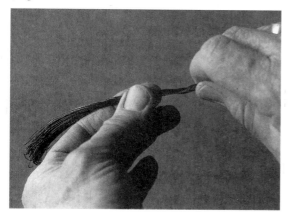

67 The strands of wire are twisted together to form the trunk.

68 Branches are formed by twisting together fewer strands of wire.

69 Branches are trimmed to the required length.

70 PVA glue is applied to the tree and flock powder sprinkled on.

71 The tree trunk after flocking.

72 Painting the tree with matt enamel.

73 Applying the foliage.

74 The finished tree.

the model as you apply the foliage, bearing in mind the three-dimensional form of the tree. Tiny pieces which collect when the material is stretched may all be used, keeping waste to the minimum. As the foliage layers grow, you may have to use tweezers to insert subsequent pieces of material.

- Stretch out fine steel wool thinly and apply to the branches as before in irregular pieces. Then spray the foliage with matt varnish from an aerosol can in small areas, and quickly, before the spray can dry, sprinkle on green flock powder.
- Another material that has interesting possibilities is *Oasis*, a firm green-coloured urethane foam used as a base for flower arrangements. It is available in blocks from florists and garden centres, and can easily be crumbled to the size of particle required. These can be applied to pre-glued branches as described previously, and give a good representation of foliage.

Whichever method is used, once the glue has set trim back the foliage to give the desired shape. You can give the effect of a flowering tree, or the formation of new leaves, by sprinkling a very sparing amount of suitably coloured flock over the completed tree.

Drill a hole in the baseboard or scenery to take the base of the trunk. Apply a generous amount of pva glue to the hole and push in the tree firmly. If necessary use a small paint pot or other suitable object to prop the tree vertically while the glue dries, and check from time to time that it has not started to lean.

When completely dry use a brush to apply a small amount of PVA glue around the base of the trunk. Sprinkle on some scatter material with a spatula to cover the junction. A touch of paint around the base may be necessary to complete the model.

When placing trees on the layout a random approach will generally prove best. Trees do not generally occur in rows unless they have been so planted, for example along a roadway or in an orchard. Groups of trees usually have the taller trees near the centre; and the colour on adjacent trees can vary. Generally the grass below the spread of big trees tends to be thinner, sometimes with soil showing through, and fallen leaves may also change the colour of the grass. A few dead trees devoid of foliage look effective, and fallen tree trunks made of suitable twigs can be added. You might even depict an area at the edge of a wood where felling has taken place: only the tree stumps, a few branches and sawdust remain to show where the trees once stood.

Water

A stretch of water in some form or other provides an additional interest to the layout, and has the advantage of introducing a number of new possibilities for modelling. A canal may include a lock scene, rivers may be crossed by bridges, harbours will need boats, cranes and so on. Each of these will form little centres of activity, with people going about their business, all adding to the overall realism of the layout.

Water is not often found in a state of absolute calm, except perhaps in the sheltered conditions of a canal or a lock. In this case glass is a suitable material, cut roughly to the shapes needed and sprayed on the underside with a mixture of blues, greens and yellows, using car aerosols. Apply small amounts of spray, mixing the colours while wet, until the desired result is obtained. When dry, lay in place and use the panels of material which form the banks of the canal to hold the glass in place, screwing through to the baseboard just beyond the edges of the glass. Bear in mind, however, that glass is breakable, and if your layout is to be portable then perhaps it would

75 The water in this canal is made of a sheet of glass sprayed a greeny-brown on the underside. The canal boat was scratchbuilt by the author.

be best to substitute perspex. Details such as the water squirting through the badly-fitting lock gates can be modelled in cellulose filler and painted in to match the main water colour, leaving a good amount of white foam showing through.

For calm water, which is rather more transparent (although unlikely in the case of the canal!), details of the water bed can be modelled in plaster and then painted in a variety of colours to represent various depths and materials. Add small pieces of gravel, pieces of foliage and other objects before laying clear glass or perspex on top.

Another method of creating a slightly less

calm effect is to paint the below-surface scene on a fairly flat surface, and then to cover it with thick-gauge clear plastic sheeting. Before the surrounding banks or buildings are applied at the water's edge, fix down the plastic sheeting with drawing pins, inducing a slight warp to the material so that reflections will be distorted. This can be highly effective in the appropriate conditions.

A river bed can be modelled in cellulose filler and painted as before to give the effect of different depths, sand banks and so on. A host of readily available materials may be added: small stones, sand, lichen, foliage – even litter. You may wish to model a flattened, muddy bank where cattle come to drink. Add a bridge if desired, and then paint the whole with a generous coat of gloss varnish to seal the surface. When the varnish has dried, pour over the whole river a further quantity of gloss varnish, the more the better, although several layers are better than one single thickness. You will find the varnish flows around the stones, leaving some projecting above the surface, and achieves a realistic rippling effect with considerable depth. It is, of course, essential that you block off any places where the varnish could escape before you begin this stage of the work.

This method, while being effective, is fairly expensive as you may have to use up to a litre of varnish. However, to some extent, the result seems to be proportional to the cost. An even more expensive, but more realistic, method is to use casting plastic, a clear acrylic material, in place of varnish. The liquid plastic and its hardener are mixed and poured over the river bed in a number of layers – keep the river fairly shallow in the interests of economy. An excellent impression of depth is given, and the final result is well worth the cost. It is important to follow the manufacturers' instructions and to allow each layer to harden fully before applying the next. If an excess amount of hardener is added to the final layer, the accelerated hardening causes small ripples to form, which enhance the completed effect.

Hedges and walls

The most commonly used material for representing hedges is sponge, cut or broken into small pieces and painted if necessary after being fixed to the model. However, on its own, it does not present a very authentic appearance, and improved results can be obtained by your glueing on pieces of scenic dressing, dyed lichen or foliage, pushing in tiny twigs here and there, and varying the colour from place to place.

Many country hedgerows, particularly where they follow the contours of sloping ground or enclose roads, are grown above stone walls. Where the horizontal layer method of building up the landscape has been used, this method of covering up the edges of layers is useful: break up a few wine bottle corks and spin them in a liquidiser for a moment or two. The resulting small pieces should be about the right scale size to represent stones used in walling. Take each piece in a pair of tweezers and dip it into pva glue, then lay it against the contour edge. It sounds a laborious exercise, but it is surprising how quickly the wall grows. The cork, being light, stays neatly in place and this helps progress a great deal. Leave some places with only a course or two of stones, and in others model a break where the collapsed stonework lies in a pile in front of the wall. When the stonework is complete add the hedge, which can either be as already described, or made of teased-out scenic dressing, small pieces of twig and scatter material glued on. The height of the hedge should vary, and in places should dip down to cover the edge of the horizontal base layers where only a few courses of stone have been laid (see figure 76).

There are a number of other ways of representing stone walls. Dry stone walls can be made by your glueing together small pieces of real stone or gravel instead of cork. Another good method is to cut a long strip of thick card about $\frac{3}{16}$in (4 to 5mm) wide, and then cut each strip into random lengths between $\frac{3}{16}$ and $\frac{3}{8}$in (4 and 10mm). The card used to back writing pads is suitable, and is often the right shade of brown or grey, which will save painting. Lay the pieces in flat courses, using tweezers to dip them into pva glue, and manipulate them into position. The work goes quite quickly, and the little inaccuracies of line enhance the general effect. You may wish to finish off the wall with a vertical capping of pieces all cut about $\frac{3}{16}$in (4mm) long. Paint the wall, if necessary, when complete, adding touches of different brown or grey here and there (see figure 77).

76   The granulated cork stonework and lichen hedge mask the edge of a step in the fibreboard contours.

77 (*Below*) The card stone wall is being hastily rebuilt by the men who knocked it down with their tractor. The ploughed field is made of corrugated cardboard.

Peco texture compound or Das Pronto are modelling clay products which give good results. They can either be cut into individual blocks from a long strip for separate laying, or simply rolled out into the shape of the wall and the pattern of stonework scribed or stippled on with a sharp instrument. Where thickness is unimportant, such as in a retaining wall against a bank, cut a piece of card to the shape of the wall and apply a thin layer of modelling compound. It is advisable to coat the card first with pva glue in order to ensure that the modelling compound does not come adrift. The joints in the stonework can then be scribed or stippled on as before, or pressed in with a thin piece of card.

Allan Downes uses a realistic semicircular stone capping on some of his models. A piece of model compound is rolled into a thin cylinder, which is then sliced lengthways down the middle. Each half is then cut into thin slices, and these small half-discs are glued to the top of the wall.

Bushes and low ground cover

Scenic dressing or pieces of dyed lichen are the most obvious choice for small bushes which might occur on your grass landscape. Larger ones may be constructed in a similar way to the method described for making trees, but on a much smaller scale. For ease of handling, leave a proportionally large twist of wire below the branched part of the bush, which will eventually be pushed into a fixing hole. About ten or twelve strands of wire are sufficient, and you can simply spray these matt black rather than apply flock powder.

Reeds can be made from sisal string or bristles from an old brush. Paint or spray these before cutting them to size, or perhaps leave them a natural colour. Cut them roughly to length in bunches, then dip the tips into contact adhesive. Paint the same adhesive

on to the area to be covered – either grassland or water – and when completely dry apply the reeds in small clumps, and you will find that they remain standing vertically.

Gardens

Flower beds can be made in the same way as grass cover by brushing diluted pva glue on to the base in the shape desired and then sprinkling on brown flock powder or scenic dressing. The surrounding grass areas can be added. When dry, remove the excess material and glue down small patches of model foliage or lichen in a range of greens and yellows. Sprinkle on coloured flocks and give the impression of individual flowers by applying tiny spots of paint. A formal garden with a pond can be constructed using one of the techniques described for water, and you may wish to make a rockery using real pieces of stone.

Farms

A ploughed field can be represented quite effectively by glueing down a sheet of corrugated cardboard (with the corrugations exposed) and coating it in the usual way with brown flock powder or scenic dressing. Use tiny scraps of dyed lichen to depict an emerging crop, or foliage of similar colour dipped into pva glue and applied in rows to the ploughed field. Remember to enclose the field with a hedge or fence, and to leave an uncultivated border around the ploughed earth.

78 Part of the town gardens, showing the war memorial and rockery.

Fencing

You are likely to have a variety of fences on your layout, beginning with those that enclose the railway itself, for in Britain, at least, there is a statutory requirement that these be provided. While the fences used around station buildings themselves were usually a distinct style, those found in remote areas varied tremendously. It would be difficult to list every type, but some of the more commonly encountered ones are described.

Post and wire

The wire strands used in a post and wire fence are probably too fine to be modelled accurately, and even if you did manage to tension the four or five wires properly, the fence would be too fragile to survive for long. It is probably acceptable to insert the posts at the correct spacing and leave the wires to the imagination. The same argument applies to telegraph poles, which usually carry wires of a similar gauge.

Post and rail

The posts can be made from thin wood strips which would be up to 2mm square to 4mm scale. They should be 3ft 6in to 4ft high (14–16mm) and spaced 8ft to 10ft apart (32–40mm). The three or four rails can be either 1mm thick wood strip 1.5–2mm wide, or similarly sized card. Where the fence covers flat ground the rails can be in fairly long lengths, but uneven ground will require the strips to be fitted between individual posts. Use contact adhesive to prevent the rails from sliding down the posts immediately after positioning. Paint black, white or brown on completion.

POST AND WIRE

POST AND RAIL

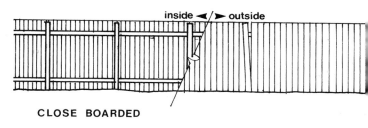

CLOSE BOARDED

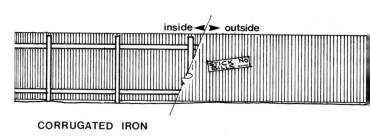

CORRUGATED IRON

79 Common types of fence.

Close boarded

This consists of posts as before but at rather closer centres, 6 to 8ft (24–32mm). Horizontal rails are attached near the top and bottom of the posts and then vertical strips of card no more than $\frac{1}{16}$in (2mm) wide are glued to the rails side by side, or slightly overlapping. The fence should be painted black or brown to represent creosote. One or two boards set skew help to reinforce the impression of realism.

Corrugated iron

Instead of close boarding, a corrugated iron cladding can be used. Some thin metal foil is required, such as the sealing foil used in larger cans of instant coffee or cocoa. Cut this into strips of, say, 6ft (24mm) and fasten one end down to your work surface with masking tape. Using a straightedge and a scribing tool such as a blunt screwdriver, score lines across the width of the foil very close together to represent the corrugations. Glue the corrugated iron to the horizontal rails and paint on the finishing colour, which may include some areas of rust showing through. A few cuts in the sheeting near the top and bottom with the edges bent over add to the effect of dilapidation if required.

Plastic

Plastic fence sections, representing railway company outlines, are available from a number of manufacturers. There are also some superior models of 4mm scale fencing including barbed wire, mesh and slat-and-wire in etched brass from John Piper (Accessories) Ltd.

Figures

The inclusion of human figures on the layout does much to define scale and bring it all to life. Merit produce fully detailed and coloured figures, and Dapol make a similar but unpainted range. Some are supplied attached to sprue, which makes painting them a good deal easier. If they are provided with bases, these are best cut off before painting. The figures can be set in position on the model by applying a dab of pva glue to the feet and standing them in position, propped up by small paint pots or something similar until dry.

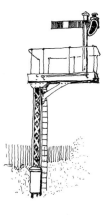

5 Buildings

There was a time when the only buildings associated with a model railway were those that were essentially part of the railway system, such as stations, signal boxes, and goods sheds. These did little to enhance any attempt at realism, being generally out-of-scale and poorly designed models. More recently, the importance of the scenic effect has demanded that far more attention be paid to these elements. Manufacturers have not been slow to take advantage of this situation and there is now a wealth of commercially produced kits and building materials, many of excellent quality. Scale and realism are now essential factors in their design, and there is frequently a satisfying degree of attention to fine detail. The range covers the most popular gauges, and extends to every imaginable type of building that might be encountered on a model railway layout. As well as catering for kit modellers, there is a variety of materials to delight the scratchbuilder, enabling him to create structures that represent every degree of complexity, from simple coal staithes to elaborate town buildings.

There appear to be only a few ready-made buildings available, probably because manufacturers appreciate that there is much satisfaction to be gained from self-assembly, however limited this might be. But for those who need complete buildings, *Gallia Reproductions* market a range of well-detailed resin-cast structures such as houses, churches, barns and ruins to suit Z, N and OO gauges.

These are supplied ready painted, although there is still scope to add creepers and lichen if you require an element of individuality. Also available are some accessories, including stone walling, chimneys and bridges. The manufacturers suggest that using buildings of smaller scale towards the back of the layout creates an illusion of perspective, which is a useful hint to bear in mind for other components of the model such as trees and hedges.

For the inexperienced, attempts at the construction of simple kits of few parts will do much to encourage initially. It is easy to correct mistakes, and set aside irretrievably botched buildings for cannibalising when you have progressed to scratchbuilding models to your own design. As in most other aspects of this hobby, a study of kits, materials and techniques illustrated in modelling magazines provides much useful information as well as engendering enthusiasm.

Tools

Not only will you need a selection of suitable tools for modelling your buildings, but also a place to carry out the work. Those who are fortunate enough to have a small workshop or modelling room have the advantage of being able to stop their labours and recommence at a later time knowing that nothing will have been disturbed. It might be possible to set aside a part of your layout room for modelmaking, the main requirement being that adequate light is available on the work surface.

Much of what you do will involve cutting through sheets of card and plastic and a suitable surface for this exercise is important. You will need to protect the work surface in some way, yet a hard material such as sheet aluminium or a plastic laminate will wear out the cutting edge very quickly. Most modellers have their own preferences, but you will find a good compromise is a sheet of hardboard about 2ft × 1ft 6in (600mm × 450mm). It will in time start breaking up as the number of surface cuts increase, but it is a relatively cheap material to replace.

A word about using those cutting tools. Having determined the line on which to cut, press a metal straightedge down firmly against the line with the fingers of one hand and draw a knife down the straightedge with the other. As you will be concentrating on the accuracy of the cut there is a very real danger that some of the fingers holding the straight edge might project into the path of the knife. Always make absolutely certain that your fingers are well clear before beginning the cut, or your modelmaking capacity may become somewhat diminished.

You will need:

- A large craft knife for thick or heavy work, and a modelling knife for the finer detail. A scalpel is useful for really delicate work.
- A metal ruler or straightedge, at least 12in (300mm) in length. Some of these have a square incorporated, otherwise you will need to have a separate tool for determining right angles.
- A set of needle files including round, tapered round, square, triangular and flat ones.
- Several grades of sandpaper or emery cloth, which will be used in conjunction with needle files.

- Pointed and blunt-end tweezers which must be checked to see that the jaws meet positively.
- A large and a small pair of scissors for cutting irregular shapes.
- Needle-nosed pliers for wire bending and jobs too heavy for tweezers.
- A small pair of wirecutters.
- A set of fine drills. These can either be fitted into the chuck of a pin vice, or used with a miniature electric drill. Another use for the latter is to fit it with a mandrel and corundum disc to make rail-cutting very much easier.
- A small saw, such as a junior hacksaw. Some modelling knives have sawblades which can be fitted into the handle.
- A small bench vice, which is very useful to grip objects being cut or shaped.
- A few bulldog clips or clothes pegs to hold items while glue dries.
- A scale, or perhaps the ruler mentioned earlier, marked off in millimetre divisions, 6in (150mm) long. It is also useful to have a scale handy to the layout, which gives direct readings to the gauge you have chosen. This can be made with a stout strip of card or Plasticard. For OO gauge, mark 4mm divisions and calibrate the scale in feet. Adhesive tape can be stuck over the completed scale to protect the markings.
- A set of paint brushes, varying in quality and size. The best will be used to add fine detail, while the indifferent ones will serve to spread adhesive.

Adhesives

You will find that the most useful adhesive for building your layout, whether it be baseboard construction, scenery modelling or structures, is white PVA glue such as Evo-Stick *Resin W wood adhesive*. By far the most economical size is 1 litre, and the glue will remain usable for some years if kept well sealed. For convenience you can withdraw a small amount for day-to-day use and keep this in a plastic hand-lotion bottle or one of the smaller adhesive containers, most of which have a useful spout. Use a suitable stopper to prevent the glue from setting in the nozzle, such as a brass or stainless steel nail or screw. This glue has the advantages of not setting too quickly and being almost invisible when dry because of its matt finish.

For joining Plasticard and other poly-styrene plastics, use a polystyrene solvent. This is a welding agent which acts by partly dissolving the surfaces to be joined. The two parts are held together and a small amount of the solvent touched to the join by means of a brush. Capilliary action causes the liquid to be dispersed over the areas in contact, and a solid bond is formed in a matter of seconds. Care must be taken not to touch the freshly joined plastic, or fingerprints will become embossed on the surface.

Metal can be very securely bonded to other materials with an epoxy resin glue. This is a two-part adhesive which after being mixed must be used quickly, as the initial set takes place within a few minutes.

Materials

For building models you will need:

- Card, the most commonly used material, which can be obtained in a variety of thicknesses and qualities from art shops, stationers and drawing office suppliers. It is best not to use cheap, thin card as this tends to buckle. Photographic mounting card is excellent, although fairly expensive. Unless you have some doubling-up construction in mind it is probably best not to use card less than 1mm thick.

- Plastic card (polystyrene sheet), an alter-native material to consider, which gives an excellent finish. It, too, is available in a variety of thicknesses, and it can be easily cut and shaped. It can be readily joined using a solvent glue. The transparent sheet can be used for windows, with the glazing bars painted or scribed on. The material is also available in a number of embossed forms representing brickwork, stone wall-ing etc, which look very realistic when painted.

- Polystyrene extrusions, a new alternative, in the form of strips, rods, tubes, girder sections and so on.

- Moulded polystyrene which represents cobblestones, pavings, corrugated as-bestos, wood fencing, roofing tiles and a variety of useful surfaces (marketed in the Wills *Finecast* series).

- Wood in the form of strips, which is available from some model shops. Balsa is the most commonly available, but is not really suitable unless concealed in the construction, as the grain is very coarse. Lime or obeche strips are far more suitable, and have many uses, including fencing and bridge construction.

- Printed papers representing many types of brick, stonework and roofing materials in accurate colours which can be found in most model shops. While this can give a good representation of brickwork, you must remember that for more textured surfaces which can be examined at close range it is preferable to use a material which reflects more accurately this texture. (Good examples are those marketed by Prototype Models and Superquick.)

- Aluminium and brass tubing, available at some model shops in a good range of sizes. This can be used for pipework or columns on buildings.

- Dental plaster, useful for modelling stone-work, while plaster fillers can give realistic textural effects.

- Clay, another material which can be moulded to represent surface textures (some examples being *Pecoscene* texture modelling compound, *Pyruma* fire cement and *Das Pronto* modelling clay; all of these harden in time without the need to fire them).

You will undoubtedly discover a host of other modelling materials as the need for them arises, items which you would otherwise have discarded as junk. You can adapt pieces of wire, scraps of metal and plastic, broken toys and many household items past their prime to fill the demands of the layout.

Card kits

There is now available a range of good-quality card kits covering such a variety of building types that one is tempted to set aside scratchbuilding, at least initially, in the interests of having some buildings on the layout at an early stage. Most of these are quick and easy to construct, and the manufacturers have taken considerable trouble to allow even the relatively inexperienced to build satisfyingly realistic models.

Perhaps the best and most well-known of these in the OO guage range are the card kits marketed by *Superquick*. These fall into three categories: station buildings; town and country buildings; and low relief town buildings. The kits are printed in full colour on thick card, and all cuts and fold-lines are made during manufacture, so that parts need only to be released by your using a sharp modelling knife. Clear plastic windows are included, as well as straightforward instruction notes. The sheets are assembled ingeniously, with economical use of card, and the design of the buildings has been handled

with architectural sensitivity and understanding.

Other card kits to choose from are the *Bilteezi* range (marketed by Hamblings) *Cav'ndish* and *Builder Plus*. These cover mainly OO gauge, although some N gauge models are available. The quality of card in these kits is rather thin, and to achieve a flat surface some additional internal bracing in the form of strips of card is required.

The one criticism of card kits is that their very popularity has resulted in identical street scenes being encountered again and again on layouts. However, this can be overcome with a little trouble by slightly modifying the buildings. Often the most striking feature is a name board, or a shop window display. If applying new lettering, take care not to destroy the whole effect by clumsy efforts at hand-painted signwriting. Rub-down lettering is available in a wide range of colours and sizes, and is not too difficult to apply satisfactorily. Cut a thin piece of card to the size of the panel required, paint it, and when dry add the lettering. If a shop window display is surface printed, you might consider cutting out the panel and replacing it with a piece of clear plastic, behind which a few tiny odds and ends can be displayed. Simply repainting other parts, or adding new panels of brick paper can change the appearance quite considerably. And, of course, these modifications might be your first steps towards scratch buildings of your own design.

An example of some *Superquick* buildings is shown in figure 80. This is a whole block of buildings being constructed off-site, ready to be fitted into position on the layout when complete. There are great advantages in modelling in this way, as all parts of the buildings are completely accessible, the whole group being turned around to attain a convenient working position. The base of the model is a sheet of hardboard, and printed

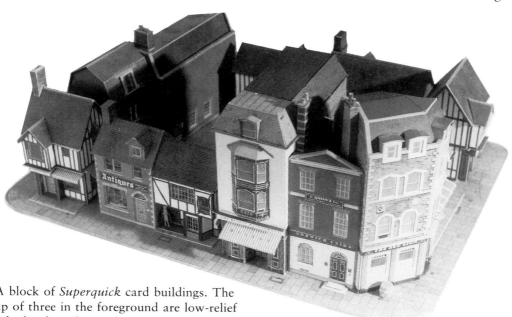

80 A block of *Superquick* card buildings. The group of three in the foreground are low-relief models that have been adapted to give greater depth by adding scratchbuilt structures behind them. Paper pavings were added to the hardboard base before glueing the buildings in place.

81 (*Below*) Modified low-relief *Superquick* buildings and a railway terminus building form part of the station complex at Culmhidon.

82 Culmhidon station, showing the *Superquick* main building, island structure and goods depot. The platforms were built to suit the trackwork configuration. The passenger bridge is a Plasticard-extended version of an *Airfix* model. The track is still to be ballasted.

paper pavements have been added before glueing the individual buildings down. Pavings, paths and flowerbeds were added in the central court, as well as a small tree. Lighting to the individual buildings was added and the wiring grouped into a suitable place to pass through the hardboard base. The group of buildings in the foreground was a low relief model, and it was necessary to add scratch-

built extensions to the back of each. These consisted of walls and roofs carefully matched to conform with the architecture of the originals. Figures, street signs and telegraph poles were finally added before transferring the model to the layout; and the result can be seen in figure 99.

Other examples of *Superquick* buildings are seen in figure 81. This shows a station building and some other low relief models which, once again, have been modified to give greater depth – this time to fill a rather awkward angle in the junction between the layout and the sloping loft ceiling.

Card kit construction usually follows a fairly straightforward procedure. You will need a sharp modelling knife, pva glue and some adhesive tape. It is important to read right through the instructions before beginning, and you should only separate from the sheet those parts which you are actually assembling at one time. Many of the identifying letters are printed adjacent to the parts concerned, and once these are separated you might experience difficulty in finding the correct locations. You might find it helpful to pencil reference numbers on the back of components. Where fold-lines have not been pre-cut, you will need to use a straightedge, and take care to follow the line accurately and not to cut right through the card. Where this does happen the parts can be rejoined by means of a adhesive tape strip on the back. Touch up the cut edges of card to match adjacent colours with a felt-tip pen.

Some of the kits for buildings of more than one storey in height do not make provision for internal floors. Much of the realism will be spoiled if you can look through the first floor windows in the front and see the ground floor windows at the back. Add card floors during construction and paint them a dark colour before fitting, in order to overcome this objection. This floor will also provide a useful stiffening to the walls. You might consider fitting a few partition walls so that the rooms inside your building do not give the impression of filling a whole floor.

Plastic kits

The popularity of plastic kits derives to a large measure from the three-dimensional quality of the mouldings. However fine the printed detail on card models, there is great satisfaction in being able to *feel* the feature of roofing tiles, brickwork and stonework; but the cost of plastic kits is several times that of the card equivalents. Matt enamel paints give excellent results on these kits, with the additional advantage that your own selection of colours will introduce individuality to the buildings. As in the case of card kits, it is often possible to interchange parts and modify them in the quest for unique models.

Ratio produce a number of railway-related structures for OO and N gauge, including a station, signal boxes, a coaling stage, pump house, water tower and cattle dock. In each case components for these are self-coloured so that painting is not essential, but some 'dirtying' and variation in the colouring is

83 GWR signal box from a pre-coloured plastic kit by *Ratio*, modelled on the prototype at Highley, Severn Valley Railway. (*Courtesy of Ratio Plastic Models Limited*)

84 This OO gauge signal cabin kit by *Springside Models* makes use of a cutaway section to show the considerable detailing within. (*Courtesy of Peco Studios*)

recommended to give that final touch of realism.

Wills Finecast have a similar range of 4mm scale structures, once again self-coloured so that painting is optional. A weighbridge, coal bunkers, coalyard, forecourt filling station and taximans' resthouse are included in the range, together with a delightfully well-detailed Victorian gent's toilet. There is also a sawtooth-roofed engine shed, a cottage and a barn, as well as some useful parts for bridge construction.

Airfix have a range of OO gauge railway-associated structures such as platforms, canopies, engine sheds, water towers, tunnel mouths and bridges, while *Hornby* markets a

85 An authentic-looking water tower constructed from a *Ratio* kit. (*Courtesy of Ratio Plastic Models Limited*)

86 A 4mm boiler house kit by *Ratio* provides scope for detailing all the outside clutter associated with this type of building. (*Courtesy of Peco Studios*)

87 This goods shed by *Ratio* is based on a prototype trader store used in the early 1950s. The kit has been designed to give some flexibility and can be extended by the use of additional parts. (*Courtesy of Ratio Plastic Models Limited*)

88 An N gauge locomotive servicing depot kit by *Ratio*. (*Courtesy of Peco Studios*)

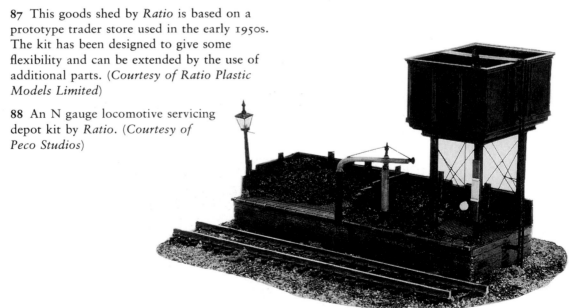

similar range with clip-together components which are suitable for beginners. The *Peco* range of lineside kits covers both OO and N gauges.

Apart from the British-manufactured kits covered so far, there are a wealth of plastic kits from European manufacturers, which follow the Continental prototypes, either in HO or N gauge. The railway-related buildings are of course unsuitable for use on British prototype layouts; but many industrial and commercial structures can be used either as they stand or with minor modifications. The manufacturers include Faller, Heljan, Herpa, Jouef, Kibri, Lima, Pola and Vollmer.

The construction of plastic kits is even more simple than the procedure for card models. The same points need to be watched:

read the instructions right through before starting, and do not separate the components from the identifying numbers on the sprue until they are needed. Use a sharp modelling knife to detach the parts cleanly, and you should check that adjoining pieces fit together properly before joining them. Use a polystyrene solvent and take care not to get the solvent on finished surfaces, or to touch them if this does happen. Where painting is required, you will obtain a much better result if adjacent pieces that differ in colour are painted before assembly. Before finally painting the completed model, fill any crevices between components with a plastic filler.

90 (*Overleaf*) A group of farm buildings constructed on the *Linka System*. This makes use of a range of flexible moulds in which wall and roof sections can be cast in plaster, and the subsequent linking together of the units allows an infinite variety of realistic building types of all sizes to be made. (*Courtesy of Linka System*)

89 An OO gauge platelayers hut kit, complete with scale tools, by *Coopercraft*. (*Courtesy of Peco Studios*)

Hybrid card and plastic kits

Prototype card kits are particularly interesting as they cover (as the name suggests) prototypes of actual structures. These include models in the N, OO and O gauge range, all beautifully detailed and with realistic colouring. The newer kits include plastic moulded parts for all finer details. *Prototype* draw attention to the fact that as a good deal of prefabrication was used in the construction of railway buildings, so in the same way their kit parts may be interchanged to some extent in order to create variations from the original. *Peco* market hybrid card/plastic kits as well, in their *Manyways* OO/HO series. The printed pre-cut card walls take advantage of the subtle detail of brick, stone and timber, while roofs, windows, doors, barge boards and the finer detailed items are in appropriately-coloured moulded plastic. The components of these kits, too, can be interchanged to give variety and individuality to the layout.

91 *Ratio* make this N gauge kit of a water tower. (*Courtesy of Peco Studios*)

Scratchbuilt models

Before any work can be started on a scratchbuilt model it will be necessary to design the building (or research the prototype) and produce a detailed scale drawing of your intentions. After making a few roughs of a fairly simple building, you may feel sufficiently confident to start setting out the components on the piece of card which will form the basis of the model; and if the luxury of a drawing board and T-square is not available to you, then you must be sure that you can produce lines precisely at right angles to one another.

Building a barn

As an exercise, you might attempt to construct the barn shown in figure 93. Set out the building and roof outlines to the dimensions shown on a piece of card at least 1mm thick. Mark the location of tabs D and E on part C, respectively $\frac{3}{8}$in (10mm) and 2in (50mm) from the gable wall; and the location of roof supports J and K. Pencil on parallel horizontal lines as guides for tiling and weatherboarding. Using a metal ruler or straightedge and a modelling knife cut partly through the thickness of the card on all the broken lines to enable you to make clean folds. (Note that one fold has to be made forward, and in this case you will need to make the partial cut on the *back* of the card.) Now cut right through on the heavy lines and remove the pieces from the sheet. Cut out the door and window openings.

Fold all the tabs at the base of walls right back and glue them down to provide extra stiffening. Take part C first and fold it to form a box, glueing the end tab so that the meeting walls are joined flush and square. Use two of the corner strengtheners inside to square up

92 One of the OO gauge layouts at the
Pecorama exhibition. The beautifully detailed
Cotswold cottages are the work of Allan
Downes. (*Courtesy of Peco Studios*)

93 An exercise in scratchbuilding. This barn
may be built to suit either OO or N gauges.

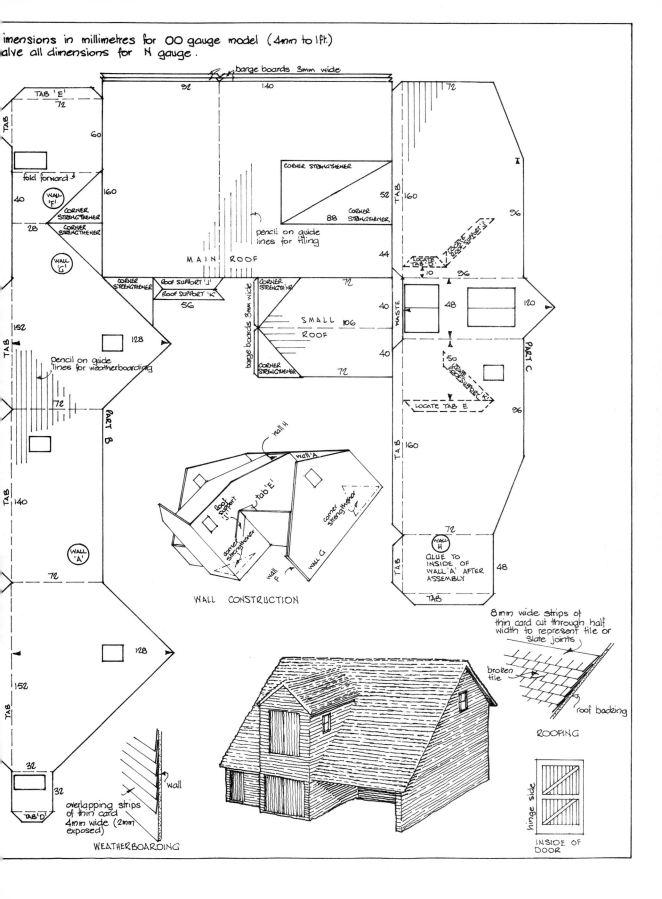

94 The seamier end of Station Road. The activity in the street does much to add realism to the scene.

the box, fitting them in the angle near the base of the back wall. Now apply glue to the back of wall F on part B, make the fold, and glue it down on to wall G to give a double thickness of card. Use a bulldog clip or a clothes peg to hold the parts together while the glue dries. Glue tabs D and E to their location points on part C, and glue wall H so that it is joined to the inside of wall A. Before the glue on this join dries, fix corner strengtheners to the inside of the angles at both ends of wall A. Glue the roof supports J and K in position on either side of the gable wall. Your basic wall structure should now resemble the illustration.

Apply glue all round the tops of the walls that will be in contact with the main roof, and the tops of the two supports J and K. Fit the main roof in position, and use pieces of masking tape to hold it while the glue dries. Repeat the process for the small roof, this time also applying glue to the roof ends that will be in contact with the main roof. Cut out the barge boards and fix them to the underside of the roof edge projections.

Doors

Glue a thin piece of card to the inside face of the door opening, and apply narrow vertical strips of card about $\frac{1}{16}$in (2mm) wide, butt jointed. If the doors are to be shown open, make them up separately with the framing and braces illustrated, and glue in position. Remember to paint the interior a dark colour if it can be seen through the doorway.

95 The 4mm layout *Heckmondwike* at the
National Railway Museum at York. This was
based on a 1930s LMS prototype, and was
designed to 'run better than any other 4mm
scale layout previously exhibited'. All trains
were to be fully and correctly signalled, and to
run at scale speeds. (*Courtesy of the National
Railway Museum*)

96 The shoring to the Georgian house and the temporary nature of the buildings on either side suggest that this street is scheduled for redevelopment in the not-too-distant future.

97 (*Below*) The addition of rubbish to the demolition site, and boxes and junk to the back yards of the adjacent buildings helps to create an atmosphere of dereliction.

Windows

Mark out the window sizes on clear Plasticard or thin acrylic sheet, allowing a few millimetres all round for fixing. Glazing bars can be scored on with a blunt craft knife. Cut out each window and fix in position with adhesive tape on the back.

Roof finish

The roof tiles or slates can be simulated by one of two methods: either cut each tile from thin card and glue separately to the roof, or make strips as shown with short cuts to represent the vertical joints between tiles. The first method appears to be excessively laborious, but in fact can be done quite quickly. Squeeze a thumbnail-sized blob of pva glue on to a waste piece of card, push the point of a sharp scalpel into one of the precut $\frac{3}{8}$in $\times$ $\frac{3}{16}$in (8mm $\times$ 4mm) tiles, touch it to the surface of the glue, and transfer it to the roof.

98 The town gardens and war memorial next to the railway bridge.

Work from the bottom of the roof towards the ridge, one whole course at a time, overlapping each subsequent course by $\frac{3}{16}$in (4mm). Follow the pencilled horizontal guide lines, but remember that the inevitable inaccuracies are desirable to give an old and weathered effect. Allow the occasional tile to slip down a little, and omit some others – but do not overdo it, or the roof will simply seem badly modelled. The strip method is considerably faster, but gives a much more regular appearance. Some tiles can be cut at an angle or removed from the strip to age the roof a little. Ridge tiles can be made by scoring down the centre of a strip of thin card about $\frac{1}{8}$in (3mm) wide, folding on the score line, and then cutting the strip into $\frac{3}{8}$in (8mm) lengths. Each ridge tile is glued so that it butts up against the next, and once again slight irregularities help to create an illusion of reality.

Walls

This is a similar procedure to roof tiling, with long strips of thin card or cartridge paper $\frac{3}{16}$in

(4mm) wide laid overlapping. Once again, work from the base of the wall upwards, using the pencilled guide lines to keep the boards horizontal. Line up the boards at the corners.

Painting the finished model

Matt enamel will probably give the best result, although it is possible to use water or oil paints. Poster paint is rather too thick. Dylon wood dyes can also be effective, and these are available in a useful range of colours. Take care that no specks of white card show though crevices in the finished paintwork. For realism it will be necessary to have some discoloured areas, and there is bound to be evidence of lichen or moss growth on the roof.

99 Part of Culmhidon town. Most of the buildings are constructed from *Superquick* card kits, many with some form of modification.

Wall textures
Brick

Brick papers give good results, but where you require a texture use embossed plastic card. This will have to be painted to give the desired shade, and perhaps you might vary the colour of some of the bricks. The pointing can be realistically shown by applying a mixture of cellulose filler to the whole surface, and rubbing most of it off before it dries. When completely dry, carefully brush off all the cellulose filler remaining on the brick face, leaving the joints neatly filled.

Another method of representing less perfect brickwork, or where brick arches and other variations are required, is to use computer card punchings. These are about the right size for OO gauge models. They must be applied one at a time to a card surface coated with pva glue, using the point of a scalpel to pick up and lay the bricks. Only a square inch or so of the card should be glued at a time, as the work proceeds rather slowly. The end result, however, is very satisfying

once the brickwork has been painted. It may not be necessary to point the bricks if the white card below shows through.

100 Detail of Culmhidon station in operation. Passengers on Platform 1 are waiting for the 4.30 express.

Stone

Stone papers and embossed plastic card can be treated similarly to their brick counterparts. Another method is to apply a layer of *Pecoscene* or *Das Pronto* to a base of thick card that has been coated with pva glue. While still soft, the pattern of stonework can be scribed on with a sharp-pointed tool; but take care not to leave a ridge of waste material on either side of the joint. Allan Downes uses a stippling action, the hundreds of closely-spaced dots being free of any ridging. Where only horizontal courses are required, as in regular coursed stonework, the joints can be pressed in with a long strip of card.

Rendering

The smooth surface of plain card does not present a very realistic appearance, and needs some additional treatment. Apply *Pecoscene* or *Das Pronto* to card in the manner described for stone, and roll with a piece of dowel for a level wood-float finish, or knead into position for rougher work. Cellulose filler or dental plaster is also suitable for use in this context. Another simple method is to sprinkle fine sand on to a card surface coated with PVA glue. When dry, tap the card to allow the excess to fall away, then paint to the required colour.

101 Part of the farm of the Culmhidon layout. The buildings are scratchbuilt. The hedge is a mixture of *Woodland Scenics* and dyed lichen, and the wall showing below is granulated cork.

102 (*Below*) A building under construction in the main street. Note the figures, the posters on the hoarding and well-used scaffolding.

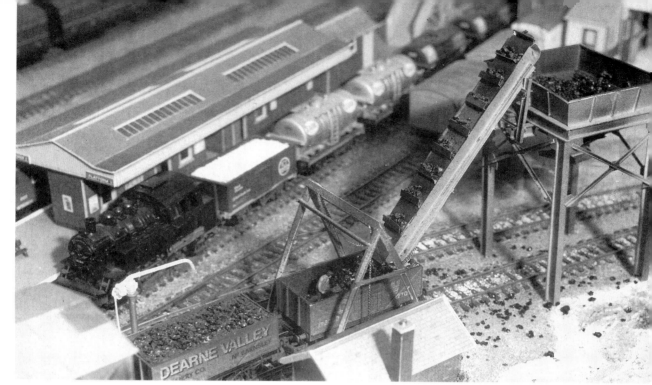

103 Coal from the wagons is shovelled on to the conveyor which deposits it in the elevated hopper. The wagons are then removed and the conveyor winched out of the way to allow locomotives to be coaled from the swivelling chute below the hopper. Note the white ash between the tracks caused by raking out the fireboxes.

104 An old timber shed with a carpenter's bench inside the open door. The roof sag was induced by the method illustrated in figure 105, and each card tile was laid individually.

Windows

The method of scoring glazing bars on to clear plastic sheet has already been mentioned. If using clear polystyrene sheet, a good effect can be obtained by dipping pieces of thread into polystyrene solvent and stretching them across the sheet. The solvent quickly bonds each thread to the plastic surface, after which, trim the free ends away with a sharp knife. The three-dimensional glazing bars so formed are quite effective.

Downesglaze is available as packs of screen-printed windows of various sizes and types, which are simply cut from the sheet and fixed behind the window openings as required. Both N and OO gauge sizes are manufactured.

Roofs

Apart from the treatment already described, roofs can be finished with embossed plastic sheets representing a number of materials.

(Wills Finecast produce a number of these, including tiles and corrugated asbestos.) For corrugated asbestos it is recommended that exposed edges of sheets are chamfered and filled with a round needle file to reduce the otherwise unrealistic thickness of the material.

Thatch

One way of producing a realistic-looking thatched roof is to use knitting wool. Construct a card base, give it a good coating of PVA glue, and then pull strands of fairly thick ply wool tightly across the roof, from eaves to eaves across the ridge. You may need more than one layer of wool to obtain the right thickness of thatch. The colour of the wool is immaterial, as it is to be stained later. When the glue has dried cut a hank of shorter strands to form the ridge piece, and glue this similarly on top of the first layer of wool so that it lies about $\frac{1}{2}$in (12mm) down on either side of the ridge. If a decorated edge is required to the ridge piece – often a zig-zag pattern is used – this should be cut by

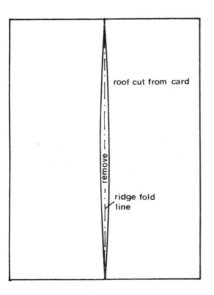

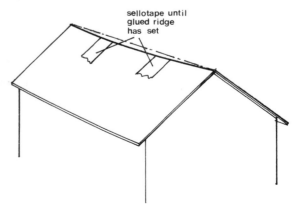

105 Forming a sag in a roof. The wider the curved piece removed, the deeper will be the amount of sag.

carefully lifting it, a piece at a time, and trimming it with sharp scissors before the glue dries. Trim the eaves. Now make a further thin application of pva glue to the whole roof, and sprinkle on flock powder. When the glue has dried completely, stain the thatch to the right colour by painting on a suitably coloured dye (such as Colron or Dylon wood dye – Teak or Dark Oak give good results).

Mounting buildings on the layout

Whether you have a single structure or a group of buildings on their own base panel to set in position on the layout, it is important that the mounting is carried out properly so that you don't waste the care you have taken in their construction. Buildings sit on foundations, and appear to grow out of the ground; and you must attempt to achieve this same appearance. Use a little filler to merge the edge of a base panel with the surrounding landscape, and apply scatter materials or flock right up to the walls of buildings. Where there is no paving at the base of a wall, there will be an accumulation of grime for the first few courses of brickwork. In the case of neglected buildings, the grass and weeds will have climbed a little way up the walls; this can be represented by the application of a little glue and a sprinkling of scenic dressing.

106 The roof of a rather derelict multiple coaling hopper, with tiling battens showing where the tiles have become dislodged.

6 Locomotives and rolling stock

For the dedicated enthusiast in the past, when few of the ready-to-run models available bore more than a passing resemblance to the prototypes they purported to represent, the only means of achieving realism was to resort either to kits or to scratchbuilding. Today, the position is greatly improved, and most of the leading manufacturers have heeded the demand for carefully and accurately detailed models. Standards are continually improving, and the materials used increasingly appropriate. Healthy competition in the production and marketing of these models is to the advantage of the enthusiast. With the tremendous diversity of prototypes and the range of popular gauges, there is little likelihood of manufacturers exhausting the possibilities of introducing new models. Commercially, they tend – understandably – to market models that are popular and likely to sell well. Nevertheless, there is an ever-increasing range of excellent locomotives, carriages and wagons available; and in many cases the same prototype has been modelled by more than one manufacturer, so that choice becomes quite a difficult task.

Kitbuilding is, however, still an attraction to many, despite the high standard of ready-to-run models. In general, the level of detail in kit components is even higher than one might find in the ready-built equivalents. Building from a kit is also a good way of gaining experience in the construction of locomotive and rolling stock models, and of course is a first step in the direction of scratchbuilding. Often modellers have the urge to enter the realms of 'kit-bashing', either because they feel the kit is not sufficiently accurate, or they wish to build a model of a prototype which itself varied from the standard production run. This adjustment of kits is another step towards scratchbuilding. The not uncommon practice of using kit parts in a scratchbuilt model appears quite legitimate, but does make the distinction between the two forms of modelmaking difficult to define.

Ready-to-run models

Probably the largest range of British locomotives and rolling stock in OO gauge is marketed by Hornby (originally known as Triang). A look through the advertisement pages of the railway magazines will show the considerable range of their products. Another well-detailed range of models is available from Wrenn, (originally the famed Hornby-

107 Part of one of the OO gauge layouts at the Pecorama exhibition. This one is fully automatic, the trains recognising the signal lights and pausing at stations and turnouts where required in a most realistic manner. The backscene panel gives an excellent impression of distance. (*Courtesy of Peco Studios*)

108 Another view of the layout shown in
figure 107. (*Courtesy of Peco Studios*)

Dublo). Both Airfix and Mainline are no longer in business, although a number of their products are still available. Some of the moulds for these two excellent ranges have been acquired by David Boyle, who markets them together with his own original model under the name of Dapol. The largest range of international models, which includes a considerable number of British outlines, is made by the Italian firm Lima.

Turning to N gauge, the British specialist in this field is Graham Farish (Grafar), with a wide range of well-detailed and reliable models. This firm produces in addition a useful range of trackside and other building kits in 2mm scale. The German firm Minitrix who specialize in continental model railways, also have a range of British outlines.

Kits

For straightforward, easily-assembled, well-designed plastic kits three manufacturers come to mind: Coopercraft, Ratio and Slaters. All three specialize in coaches and wagons, and also produce complimentary trackside building kits and road vehicles. A wide choice is available to suit the needs of the average modeller. For the specialist, exceptionally finely-detailed plastic kits requiring a little more skill are available from Dundas Models, who specialize in OO9 narrow gauge, and Ian Kirk.

Locomotive construction kits mainly in

109 Three OO gauge wagon kits by *Ratio*. (*Courtesy of Peco Studios*)

110 (*Below*) These open wagons and bolster trucks are made by *Ratio*. (*Courtesy of Ratio Plastic Models Limited*)

111 This OO-9 (narrow gauge) First World War War Department Class D ten ton dropside bogie open wagon kit is made by *Dundas Models*. (*Courtesy of Peco Studios*)

112 A block of wood cut to fit the wagon exactly has the simulated load glued to the top, and can be removed if required. The weight of the block helps the wagon to run more smoothly. Note the weathering to the wagons.

113 A *Ratio* GWR motor car van to 4mm scale. (*Courtesy of Peco Studios*)

cast white metal, suitable for those with average modelling ability, are made by Craftsman, D. J. H., M & L and Wills Finecast. In a much higher price range, aimed at the specialist, are the etched brass kits with exceptional detail, made by a host of small manufacturers who advertize in the railway modelling magazines. In order to keep the customer's options open, many of these kits contain only the parts necessary for building the body of the locomotive, the chassis and motor being purchased separately. A good model shop will advise you on the possible combinations and compatability of components. At this level of the hobby you may have to accept that, for example, the length of a locomotive body has been made a little shorter than the prototype in order to accommodate a standard chassis. This may

dismay the perfectionist, for whom the only alternative is to scratchbuild the model in order to attain the desired degree of accuracy.

Scratchbuilding

The one overriding advantage of scratch-building is that it enables you to construct something that is totally unique. To many modellers, this goal outweighs the consider-able time and effort that will be needed to produce such a model; one that will be both satisfying in the display of hard-earned craftsmanship, and authentic enough to excite the admiration of fellow enthusiasts.

Scratchbuilding covers a wide range of scales, gauges and prototypes in an equally diverse selection of materials, and is carried out by modellers possessing every degree of skill. These factors make it virtually im-possible to offer any practical guidelines, yet the basic principles are worth rehearsing.

As in all scratchbuilding work, your first task is to obtain drawings and photographs of the prototype you wish to build. Your local library may be a good starting point, or the required information may be obtained from model railway clubs or railway museums. Quite frequently detailed drawings appear in modelling magazines. If you are considering a modern vehicle, it may be possible to obtain information from British Rail – your local information office will advise you where you should address your enquiries. You may be able to take your own photographs of the prototype, although these on their own will not be sufficient.

There is also the matter of the particular period of the prototype to consider. Is your model to represent the locomotive or carriage the day it first appeared on the rails? Or were there modifications to the basic type which might be interesting to represent? What was the livery used at the stage you are going to depict? With the amount of accurate detail you are going to show on your model, there is

114 OO gauge LMS bogie coach kit (express clerestory composite) by *Ratio*. (*Courtesy of Ratio Plastic Models Limited*)

115 *Ian Kirk* produces this beautifully-detailed OO gauge kit of a Gresley period full brake LNER corridor coach, showing the distinctive teak body and curved roof. (*Courtesy of Peco Studios*)

116 (*Below*) This OO gauge third class corridor arc roof LMS carriage is made by *Ratio*. (*Courtesy of Ratio Plastic Models Limited*)

no case for vagueness here. If the information is just not available, is it worth trying to make a model of it?

Then you will have to decide on the scale and materials. For the latter, all the choice of the kit manufacturers is at your disposal – plastic in the form of styrene sheet, metal and card – in fact, anything likely that comes to hand. The cost in terms of materials will be negligible, but in terms of your time, extraordinarily expensive. The extent of your capabilities and the tools you have available will influence your choice to a larger measure. If you possess a lathe you may consider making your own chassis, turning the wheels from your own stock, or from purchased

117 *Lima's* recently-introduced well detailed BR Inter-City carriage for the modern layout. (*Courtesy of Riko International Limited*)

118 (*Below bottom*) This BR Inter-City sleeper by *Lima* shows the carriage in its most recent livery. (*Courtesy of Riko International Limited*)

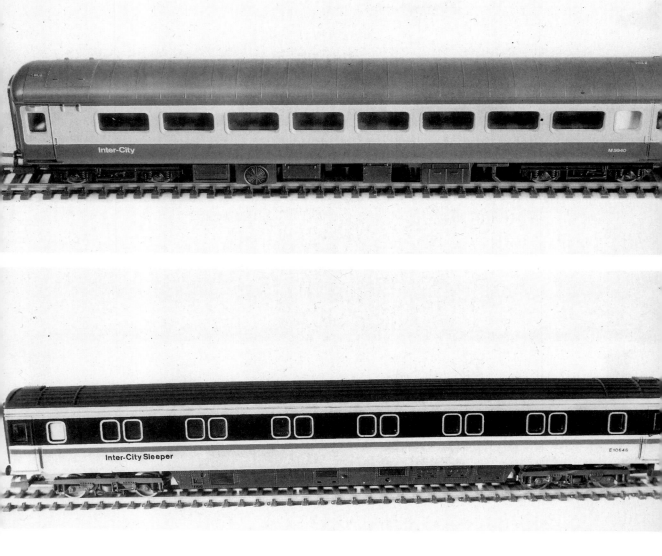

119 This OO gauge class 37 diesel Loch Rannoch is by Lima. (*Courtesy of Riko International Limited*)

castings. Otherwise, you can achieve excellent results from a superstructure of Plasticard on a suitable commercially-made chassis. Card lends itself quite well to the construction of carriages and wagons, and indeed at one stage this material was often used in kits.

Painting

The final stage in the construction process is to paint your model, and you must lavish as much care on this exercise as on every previous stage. A badly-painted but well-made model ends up as a bad model; and conversely, an excellent paint job on an otherwise rather ordinary model converts it to exhibition class.

Most professional modellers use airbrushes for all but detailed finishing. Both the airbrush and the cans of propellant are expensive items, and you must consider carefully whether your investment in these tools will give a reasonable return. If so, you might take the next step and buy a small compressor, which will certainly be more economical in the long run than an endless supply of propellant cans. (The *Devilbiss* airbrush by Humbrol is a good-quality mid-price-range item; and the same firm markets a number of other varieties.) Names of sup-

120 An accurately-detailed OO gauge model of a 1CO-CO1 class 45 diesel locomotive by *Mainline*.

pliers and prices can be obtained from the pages of modelling magazines.

The general areas to be sprayed should be covered with clear adhesive tape so that you are able to see what parts of the masking need to be cut away. The remainder of the model should be covered with ordinary masking tape – it is surprising how easily the spray mist will drift on to unprotected areas. After spraying, leave the paint to dry and harden completely before attempting to strip off the masking. Wheels and undercarriages should never be sprayed. These must be brush-painted afterwards. Take particular care in the case of pick-up wheels of locomotives, and make a careful check on completion to

ensure that these are completely free of paint.

If you use paint brushes, you should obtain good quality sable hair ones in a range of sizes from 0 to 5. Select from the better makes, which usually have a plastic tube to protect the head. Thorough cleaning in thinners and then with soap and water or detergent after use will do much to extend the life of a brush.

Both Humbrol and Precision market a comprehensive range of small cans of oil-based enamel paints which have been matched with care to prototype colours. You will also need satin and matt polyurethane varnish to use as protective coatings; and some compatible thinners.

121 *Graham Farish's* N gauge model of the class 55 diesel locomotive The Black Watch. (*Courtesy of Grafar Limited*)

122 *Coeur de Lion, a recently-introduced class 87 diesel in modern BR livery for OO gauge, by Lima. (Courtesy of Riko International Limited)*

Working on a small scale model necess-
itates the use of thin applications of paint if
fine detail is not to be lost. A second coat can
always be applied if the first does not give full
cover; but trying to remove too thick a coat is
not an easy task. Bear in mind that metal parts
need to be thoroughly cleaned with detergent
and hot water, and then primed before
painting, or the paint will tend to peel off.
Paint can usually be applied direct to plastic
models, provided that the surfaces have not
become greasy with handling during construction.

123 OO gauge 4-6-0 Royal Scots Fusilier in
LMS livery by *Airfix*.

124 (*Above right*) LMS 4-6-2 City of Glasgow
in N gauge by Graham Farish. (*Courtesy of
Grafar Limited*)

125 (*Below right*) A solidly built, well detailed,
reliable HO gauge model of a 4-6-2 German
locomotive by *Fleischmann* causes some
surprise to the workmen on this section of LMS
track.

Weathering

Applying weathering to a new model fresh from its packaging takes a degree of courage, yet the pristine appearance of a railway model certainly detracts from its authenticity on a layout. Showcase models are acceptable in that context, but for realism some evidence of service is necessary. It is not sufficient to rely on memory of weathering, and simply to apply a quick spray from an aerosol can, if this realism is to be achieved – indeed, far more harm than good may be done.

Photographs, once again, or direct observation backed up by notes and sketches, are essential if credible results are to follow. Note where rust, grime and soot collect, where poor boiler seals allow stains to form, where diesel exhausts have blackened, and even where indifferent cleaning has been carried out.

126 An OO gauge kit by *Premier (M & L)* was used to construct this model of a GWR 850 class 0-6-0 Pannier Tank Locomotive. (*Courtesy of Peco Studios*)

127 Another *Premier* (M & L) kit in white metal and etched brass of an LMS (ex LNER) 2-4-2T passenger tank locomotive. (*Courtesy of Peco Studios*)

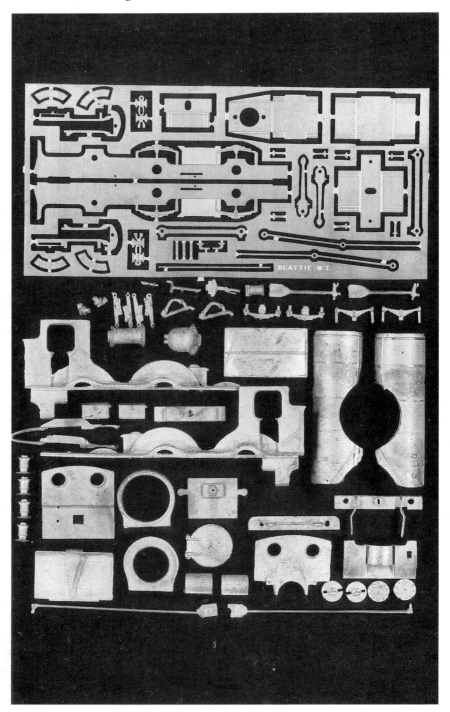

128 The contents of a locomotive kit – in this case, a 2-4-0 LSWR Beattie well tank by *Westward Models*. The etched brass components can be cut from the sheet at the top, while the remainder of the parts are white metal castings. (*Courtesy of Peco Studios*)

129 A selection of period road vehicles available from *Merit*. (*Courtesy of Peco Studios*)

130 A 4mm scale AEC Monarch lorry with flat-bed body (1933) available as a kit from *Coopercraft*. (*Courtesy of Peco Studios*)

Ideally, use a miniature spray gun, but failing this there are a number of matt aerosols in suitable colours available from model shops. Matt black, rusty red and dusty yellow are the most obvious colours to use. Mask off areas not to be included with masking tape, and apply one quick pass of the aerosol from at least 12in (300mm) away. Examine the result, and if necessary repeat the process, or change the colour. It is vital to use the spray very sparingly. You may wipe away some of the paint quickly before it dries, using a cloth dipped in thinners, to give the appearance of partial cleaning, in places such as over identification numbers. Gloss black paint sparingly applied around oiling points or the filler caps of tankers gives an effective appearance.

Suppliers' list

The majority of materials mentioned in the text are readily available from most model shops, particularly those which specialize in the field of model railways. The materials include trackwork, turnouts, foam underlay and all track-laying accesories; building kits in various forms; flock, scatter materials, scenic dressing, plastic card, and modelling clay; modelling paints and enamels; as well as locomotives and rolling stock. If you have no local model shop, you should be able to obtain your requirements through mail order services provided by many of the modelling equipment specialists, whose addresses are available in magazines such as the *Railway Modeller*. These firms publish price lists of the items stocked together with postage and packing rates.

General suppliers

Railmail
Dept RM4
65 Vicarage Road
Watford

Cheltenham Model Centre
39 High Street
Cheltenham GL50 1DY

Latching relays and electrical components

Most of the larger cities have an electrical surplus shop which can be a useful source of many of the railway modeller's requirements, and it is a worth while exercise to explore them. Failing this, a wealth of electronic components are available from:

Electromail
P O Box 33
Corby
Northants NN17 9EL

Apart from the firm mentioned above, the specific components required for the construction of the simulator unit (page 48, as well as other items such as diodes, resistors, capacitors, reed switches and wiring can be obtained either direct or by post from:

H. L. Smith & Co. Ltd
287–9 Edgware Road
London W2 1BB

Printed circuit board construction materials

The surplus shops mentioned earlier are a good source of copper laminate sheet, but this can often be obtained at other electrical component dealers. (H. L. Smith & Co. keep a supply of various sized boards.) The etching fluid, ferric chloride, is less easy to obtain. It is not normally stocked by pharmacists, but the laboratories of schools and colleges are almost certain to keep it. Alternatively, printed circuit kits, which contain the necessary chemicals and components, are available from Tandy shops, and the address of your nearest retail outlet may be obtained from the wholesalers:

Tandy Corporation (Branch UK)
Tameway Tower
Bridge Street
Wallsall
West Midlands WS1 1LA

Plaster bandage

This is stocked by most chemists, or by model shops in the form of Mod Roc. Chemists will also be able to supply you with dental plaster and plaster of paris.

Casting plastic kits

These can be obtained from some toyshops as well as being stocked by many art shops.

Other materials and suppliers mentioned in the text are listed below:

Landscaping materials

Colron
Stirling Roncraft
Chapeltown
Sheffield

Coopercraft
25 Swain Street
Watchet
Somerset
TA23 0AD

Holts Ltd
Handforth
Manchester

John Piper Accessories Ltd
(see Peco)

Building materials

Downesglaze
(see Peco)

Gallia Reproductions
(see Peco)

Hamblings Models Ltd
29 Cecil Court
Charing Cross Road
London WC2N 4EZ

Holts Ltd
Handforth
Manchester

Hornby Hobbies
Westwood
Margate
Kent CT9 4JX

Humbrol Ltd
Marfleet
Hull HU9 5NE

Linka System
Russel House
Greenwell Road
Alnwick
Northumberland NE66 1HB

Merit
(see Peco)

Peco Publications and Publicity Ltd
Beer
Seaton
Devon
EX12 3NA

Prototype Models
Matlock Bath
Matlock
Derbyshire

Ratio Plastic Models
Hamlyn House
Mardle Way
Buckfastleigh
Devon TQ11 0NS

Slaters Plastikard Ltd
Royal Bank Buildings
Matlock Bath
Matlock
Derbyshire DE4 3PG

Sundeala Board Company Ltd
Sunbury on Thames
Middlesex TW1L 5DG

Superquick
(Most model shops are agents)

Wills Finecast
(see Peco)

Rolling stock

Airfix Products Ltd
Haldane Place
Garratt Lane
London SW18 4NB

Dapol Model Railways Ltd
Queen Street
Northwich
Cheshire
CW9 5NU

DJH
Grandspot Ltd
Leadgate Industrial Estate
Lope Hill Road
Consett
Durham DH8 7RS

Dundas Models
P O Box 009
Bo'ness
Scotland EH51 9AH

Faller
(Agent) Holt Model Railways
Holt House
Caswell Bay
Swansea

Fleischmann, Märklin
M & R (*agent*)
27 Richmond Place
Grand Parade
Brighton
Sussex

Grafar
Graham Farish
Romany Works
Wareham Road
Holton Heath
Poole
Dorset BH16 6JL

Hamblings Models Ltd
29 Cecil Court
Charing Cross Road
London WC2N 4EZ

Heljan
Agent: Kittle Hobby
24 Pennard Road
Kittle
Swansea SA3 3JS

Hornby Hobbies
Westwood
Margate
Kent CT9 4JX

Ian Kirk Model Engineering
The Old Station Yard
Netherton Industrial Estate
St Monans
Fife KY10 2AT

Lima
(see Riko)

M & L
(see Peco)

Minitrix
Agent: Beatties
202 High Holborn
London WC1V 7BD

Peco Publications and Publicity Ltd
Beer
Seaton
Devon EX12 3NA

Riko International Ltd
13–15a High Street
Hemel Hempstead
Herts HP1 3AD

Vollmer, Kibri
No 4 Factory Unit
Station Yard
Bala
North Wales

Wills Finecast
(see Peco)

G. & R. Wrenn Ltd
Basildon
Essex

Lighting

Blackwell's
733 London Road
Westcliffe on Sea
Essex SSO 9ST
(for grain of wheat bulbs)

Colworth Electronics
P O Box 41
Newbury
Berkshire RG14 6HX
(for wiring and fibre optics)

Tools

Minicraft
Black and Decker
Cannon Lane
Maidenhead
Berks SL6 3PO

Swann Morton Sales Ltd
Sheffield 6
South Yorkshire

X-Acto
Stanley Tools

Cascamite wood glue, pva glue, epoxy resins, Dylon dyes, cellulose filler, steel wool, wood dyes, fire cement, adhesives and general tools are available from most hardware shops.

Scalpel blades and handles, card, cartridge paper, Letraset and modelling clay are available from art shops and drawing office suppliers

Where to see model railway displays

By far the greatest number of displays of model railway layouts are concealed in the lofts and sheds of the thousands of enthusiasts throughout the country, and are therefore rarely seen by the public. Some of these, however, occasionally appear at fairs and crafts exhibitions, or are used in conjunction with fund-raising events.

Model railway clubs, on the other hand, often have display as a primary objective as a means of raising money for the furtherance of their activities, and will be seen more frequently at larger exhibitions. The largest annual display is the International Model Railway Exhibition, usually held during Easter week in the Horticultural Halls, Westminster, London, where both private and commercial layouts may be seen. This is a good opportunity to examine and possibly buy some of the large range of new products always on show.

There are other annual exhibitions at a number of cities in Britain, notably York, at the Assembly Rooms, during Easter week; and at The Exhibition Centre, Cannon's Road, City Centre, Bristol, during May. There is also one at Derby in the Assembly Rooms, Market Place, during Easter week.

There are a few permanent layouts which may be seen at any time of the year. At York, the National Railway Museum houses a fine operating display in a gallery leading off the vast hall which contains many full-sized railway locomotives. This exhibition provides enough material to delight the enthusiast for a whole day, and is highly recommended.

Peco mount a permanent display called Pecorama, at their head office at Beer, near Seaton, Devon. Several working layouts to various scales are exhibited in a hall which is part of a large complex showing various aspects of the railways world. The whole provides a pleasant venue for a summer's day family outing. Only the exhibition hall is open during the winter months.

Some of the larger stockists of model railway equipment, such as Hamleys of London, exhibit permanent working layouts as part of their display. Many of the model towns and villages around Britain incorporate working model outdoor railways, usually to O gauge or larger. One such example is Beaconscot, near Beaconsfield, in Buckinghamshire.

The Science Museum in London also mount permanent displays.

Index

Page references in italics refer to illustrations